Time, Change, and Other Things
That Don't Fit Into Boxes

ALSO BY SHELBY KARDON

Mosaic

Time, Change, and Other Things
That Don't Fit Into Boxes

a collection of poems & prose by

SHELBY KARDON

Time, Change, and Other Things That Don't Fit Into Boxes
copyright © 2022 by Shelby Kardon.

ISBN: 979-8-21-807701-3 (paperback), 979-8-21-807702-0 (ebook)

Book design & layout by Rachel Clift. rcliftpoetry.com

First printing edition, 2022.

Shelby Kardon
@mosaic_poems

One of the many things I love about poetry is that it's slippery; it can move in between worlds, it doesn't have to offer clarity or hope or vision, it only has to make us pay attention to the world.

- Ada Limón

Introduction

Poetry is, in essence, observation — of people, of the world, of emotions and experiences, of the things that go unanswered, of the things that leave us unsettled. It's a willingness to sit in the bittersweet and take a look around. It's finding it not a luxury, but a *necessity* to use language to paint pictures, make meaning, and express and accept feelings, for better or for worse. And one thing I love most about the observational nature of writing is that it stills the chaos around us and calms the chaos within us. This collection emerged as just that. Observations, stories, emotional snapshots, and reflections of different facets of life that make it complex — heartbreaking and beautiful — all at the same time.

As a deeply feeling person in an often complicated and messy world, writing allows me to explore and unpack all that comes along with the territory of being one of the soft ones. Whether witnessing, imagining, reflecting, or most often, all of the above, the reality is, I spend a lot of time in my head. It's here where I grapple with the inherently ungraspable nature of things like time, change, love, loss, uncertainty — seemingly untamable beasts that both fascinate and terrify me. But as I navigate what it means to exist as a human along with these inescapable components of it,

one thing has become unmistakably evident. And that is that very few things about life, feelings, and people neatly fit into definitive boxes. So when we can honestly acknowledge that so much of being an authentic person is to live not in the black and white, but in the gray, all the things that seemingly don't make a lot of sense start to become a bit more clear. And in my opinion, part of truly living means examining the things that rock us to our core, admitting the uncertainties that eat at us, and shedding light on what really makes us feel something. To me, this collection reflects that.

The general assumption when a writer shares poetry is that the emotions, stories, and musings entwined in the words are entirely autobiographical. Often, people have a tendency to conclude that "I" always means the author and "you" always means one specific person. This can result in readers digesting the writing in a very black and white way — as if it's unequivocally about one specific aspect of the poet's life. And sometimes that's true. However, this collection is not that. As Nikki Giovanni once said, "I want to be clear about this. If you wrote from experience, you'd get maybe one book, maybe three poems. Writers write from empathy." Which is to say, some of these stories are my own, some are not, and some are somewhere in between. Such is art.

Many pieces in the following pages have been shared online prior to the release of this book. But now as a part of this collection, they have taken on a different life in my eyes. So, if you're reading them again, I hope they speak to you in new ways this time around. Stylistically, I played around with many different types of writing and formatting within this book. When I write, each poem tends to evolve with a certain way it's meant to be formatted. I wanted to stay true to that rather than forcing all of the pieces to fit in one specific style or format "box." So if consistency is something you're looking for, you won't find it here. Similarly, there are no sections dividing this collection into separate thematic parts. This is meant to physically emulate how life doesn't fit neatly into closed off sections any more than humans, or in this case, poems, fit into tidy boxes. The result is one big jumble of human complexity. One shade of gray spilling into another. And so it goes.

Contents

SEASONS

There is a paradoxical
comfort and discomfort
to be found in seasons —
knowing that what is here
won't last forever,
even if it feels like it will.
Like it might.
Like it could.

And it's true that
some seasons are more enjoyable than others —
a fiery warmth in frigid months,
a lonesome, icy draft amidst sweltering heat.
Whatever the temperature,
whatever the conditions,
it's easy to get caught up
in the timelessness of it all,
like we're in fact,
frozen in time,
for better or for worse.

But in the grand scheme of things,
regardless of specifics,
it's all momentary,
even when it doesn't feel that way.
And truly,
all things considered,
there is really nothing
that is certain to remain,
but for seasons,
and the knowledge
that things will change again,
and inevitably,
so will we.

WIDE OPEN

I lay with the window open wide,
a perfect parallel to my mind.
An endless expanse of space and time —
all the things that could be.

ON TRACK

"Life is like a roller coaster," he said.
Five years old, there I sat,
wide-eyed, small body snuggled into our worn, fluffy couch,
the room aglow in that warm, cozy, broken in living room way.
I watched his hands mimic the ups and downs of a roller coaster track,
innocent and unaware of how those words would ring true.

I listened,
naive, lacking foresight,
unable to really understand how
one day, my world would truly flow in that exact way —
at times gently rolling,
then eventually
giving way to
sharp turns,
steep inclines,
deep drops,
upside down loops.

No father gets everything right.
Not every nugget of wisdom lands
in a spot where it's heard.
But with this one,
he was right on track.

JUST LIKE THAT

Just like that,
things change.
Like how spring gives way to summer
sneakily,
it happens before you really
give it much thought.
You feel it first.
Then it clicks.
You're not quite ready
to move away
from the warm, dewy mornings.
Not quite ready
for the suffocating heat
that moves in
and never really leaves,
but instead lingers,
surrounding everything.

Attempts to settle comfortably
into this new thickness
are feeble, at best,
but what other choice is there?
So, you make do.
Kind of.
Until,
inevitably,
just like that,
things change.

COMING AND GOING

One season *r o l l s* into the next,
quiet, yet resolute.
The coming,
a breath of fresh air,
ushers in a refreshing *change of pace.*
The going,
persistently determined to
linger just a little l o n g e r,
reminds us of what we leave behind.

SUMMER ENDS LIKE

Your tendency to turn and run. Like a flame snuffed out, noxious smoke still lingering in the air, a stubborn heat that won't fully leave. Like your hand pulling me in, and then pushing and pushing and pushing me away. Like the last strawberry in the carton. Like the sunset fading into blackness while I fight to imprint the image into my memory for safekeeping (but I'll never get it back). Like my favorite part of my favorite song losing its spark because I've completely played it to death. Like a ship returning to harbor, the adventure over. Like time running out. Like the deepest ache that twists and shifts, but always, always returns. Like a peach pit left in my outstretched hand—greedily sucked clean of its fleshy fruit, a last remaining artifact of sweetness, now nothing but cold and hard and bare. Like a chapter ending, but bracing for the next one coming. Like the air squeezed out of my lungs, slowly, slowly, then all at once. Like rocks being piled back on my shoulders, one by one by one. Like a heart breaking…for the millionth time, but not the last time. Like curtains closing. Like rounding a corner. Like hoping for change. Like wishing for just a little longer. Like saying goodbye. Like letting it all go. Like knowing what's coming must be even better than what's gone.

YOLK

Some days I feel
like a rogue egg
escaped from the top shelf of the refrigerator,
somersaulting to its demise —
the crack of the cold, hard kitchen floor,
shell fragments everywhere,
yellow, sticky yolk
b / r / o / k / e / n
and slowly *s e e p i n g*
anywhere it can reach.

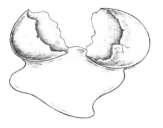

QUESTIONS WITH NO ANSWERS

All my visceral hopes and dreams
course through my body
at any given moment.
Even the ones I don't want.
Even the ones that aren't fully fleshed out yet.
I can feel them, nonetheless.
All punctuated with a question,
maybe two, often more.
Questions that lead me everywhere and nowhere.
Questions that the internet can't answer.
Questions that leave me stuck,
scratching my head when 2 + 2 doesn't add up,
and Google can't translate because
sometimes it's not about the answers.
Sometimes there is no clear or perfect translation.

Teachers always say
that it's not really the end product that matters,
but rather the *process* where all the learning takes place.
I'm a teacher.
I know this.

Yet still, I find myself
whisper-screaming wonderings
into the void
as I assiduously type them
into my trusty search bar:

> *How many forms of whiplash are there? How do you know when you've crossed over from hope into denial? At what point does optimism become foolishness? Where do you draw the line between patience and persistence? When do you surrender to the questions because the answers never come? What do you do when logic fails and feelings prevail, but, "That's just not the world we live in?" How do you know if you're weathering a storm or if you **are** the storm? At what point does too much become not enough? How do you know when a period is the start of an ellipsis...or the end of a sentence? How do you know when you've been leveled or you're just preparing to level up?*

I type,
keep typing,
click search,
wait,
wait,
wait,
keep waiting,
but still the answers just won't load.

FLEETING

It's beautiful and then it dies.
The colors striking enough to make us stop —
mid-step,
w o n d e r s t r u c k,
as we watch leaves *turn*
in the blink of an eye,
abandon ship,
and surrender to the fall
one
   by
     fading
       one.

QUIET TRANSISTIONS

It's the quiet transitions that speak the loudest, isn't it?
The silent recognition of,
"We were here, and now we're here,"
before there's even time to adjust.
It's the subtle shifts
that send wheels spinning —
on a run, folding laundry,
lost in thought while washing dishes,
soap suds covering fingertips,
water drenching our shirt from the sink edge,
and then it hits —
and we're just there,
standing alone
with soaked through cotton
and the realization of how much has changed.

THE GREAT ESCAPE

It's been a while since we escaped the real world.
And by we, I mean I,
but you came with me, didn't you?
It's been a while since
I was unexpectedly propelled into this
alternate universe,
my insides split open,
all my wildest dreams spilled out,
unruly and untamable,
messy and marvelous,
all over the goddamn place.
I reveled in the reverie.
And you did too.

It's been a while, and I still don't want to leave.
It's been a while, and I'm still trying
painstakingly, *fruitlessly*, **impossibly**
to find all the original scraps of "reality"
and put them back together.

But the thing is,
when you escape,
when you leave a place
and fall in love
with another world,
you come back with pieces of it still on you.
A sanguine scent stuck to your skin.
Film reel fragments flickering
and fading as you try to
both **hold on** and *let go*

.

.

.

ultimately failing to do either.

Obviously,
the return trip of any getaway
is bound to come with
its own brand of disappointment.
Once past the turbulence
and altered flight paths,
once landed safely back in the world you left behind,
everything is colored slightly differently.
Nothing is quite the same.
And maybe it's not the world itself that's changed
so much as it's you,
with all your secrets whispered to the wind,
and your mosaic memories that remain
and remind you of what is possible.

ROGUE THREADS

When you lose something,
you don't lose it all at once.
More like it unravels *c o n t i n u o u s l y*
for however long it takes
for all the threads to *u n t a n g l e*
from around your heart,
and from around your fingertips,
and don't forget the ones
looped around every last inch of your skin.

It's like each strand that pulls away
takes more and more with it,
leaving nothing but gaping holes and frayed edges
that you attempt to grasp,
attempt to tie back into some makeshift thing that *could* work.

The painful truth that's hard to swallow
is that despite your efforts, you *know*
it's all slowly slipping away,
sure as each rise and set of the sun.
The firmest of grips won't undo what's been done.
But you try anyway.
The distance g r o w s,
a cavern opening inside you —
and nothing seems the right shape to fill it.
But you try anyway.

Call it timing, call it practicality, call it fate,
call it what you want,
but at the end of the day,
when you lose something,
you just lose it —
and you're left with nothing to show for it
but some rogue threads
dangling from your fingers that are somehow,
still
   hang-
      ing
         on.

WHY BOTHER?

Because we're alive. Because what else are we doing here? Because we're meant to feel. Because when we find the things that light us up, we should run toward them, not away. Because we're blood and flesh and bone, pulsing and thrumming with life, and every bit of it is a miracle. Because we're here. Because we could be gone tomorrow. Because something is better than nothing. Because perfection is an illusion. Because have you ever felt electricity in your body? Because music and poetry and sunrises and sunsets. Because full moons and starry skies. Because connection. Because magic does exist. Because chaos. Because love. Because there is so much beauty to be found. **Because.** Just because. *Just because.*

DUALITY

Myth: "It can't be both."

Oh, but how wrong that is.
Because it can and *it is.*
And we can choose to ignore it all we want,
but the reality is,
we are all so very much *this*
and so very much *that* —
yes, **BOTH**, at the same time.

We're broken, but whole.
Stuck while moving, moving while stuck.
Here, but also there.
Grateful, yet wanting.
Content, yet unsettled.
Full, yet so, so hungry.

We're both loving and hurting.
Truth and deception.
Partners and strangers.
Deeply happy and deeply sad.
We're clear blue skies and the thickest of thunderclouds,
but rainbows there if you keep your eyes open.
We're both soft insides and sharp, jagged edges.
Open windows and closed doors.

We are light and dark
and everything in between,
with all of its brightness and all of its shadow.
Because it's both/and —
yesterday, today, tomorrow, and forever —
always has been, always will be.
Both.

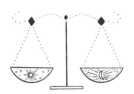

WAVES

It might be
inconvenient
to feel this way.
In fact,
I know it is.
This is not the ideal
time,
place,
or circumstance
for this wave to surge upon me.

And yet,
here it is,
crashing,
fast and fierce,
and I'm here,
confused,
scared,
and unsure
how to navigate this riptide.

The truth is,
there is no map
that will lead me through it.
There is no magic lifeboat
that will gently deliver me to shore.
There is just me
and this wave.
All I can do is
ride it out.

THAWING

Radio silence
drowns out the sound
that used to be your voice.
It's deafening,
enough to make me scream.
It thunders over
the soundtrack of my
seconds,
minutes,
hours,
days,
until it becomes
part of the background —
familiar,
normal,
expected.

Within this vacuum
exists a tension
more tremendous
than either of us would like to admit.
A tautness that is both
a stoic protection of ego
and an obstacle
standing in the way
of peace.

I drown in this silence,
pretending that
you're in the water flailing too.
I don't know this for sure, of course.
But in between my thrashing,
I urge myself to focus on
a glimmer of light in the distance.
A warmth with

the potential to subtly thaw this ice.
Baby steps, at best.
But a promising shift that
inches me along.

MOLASSES

Emotion drips
with blatant disregard
like molasses spilled
from the top shelf of the pantry.
Thick and syrupy,
somehow,
some way,
it manages to land on
literally everything
on the way down.

Dark, sticky drops
plopped
in the most unlikely of places
continue to surprise me,
while I can't help but note
that its reach is
something to be both
marveled at
and maddened by.

It takes what feels like
an eternity
to attempt to get things
free of residual stickiness,
only for me to turn and find
yet another
brown, goopy puddle
in need of attention.

THINGS THAT REMIND ME OF MY SOFTNESS

Nostalgia. Christmas in my childhood home. The smell of Mom's shampoo. Mountains of red and white starlight peppermints stashed next to Dad's bed.

The iron grip of a scared child. The reminder that I was her. That I am her.

"Forever Young" by Rod Stewart. "Let It Be" by The Beatles.

Birthdays. Old photographs. Seasons changing. Concrete reminders of the ever-quickening passage of time.

Possibilities. Dashed hopes. Shattered perceptions. Goodbyes.

The first crisp of fall. Sweatshirt weather. The crunch of leaves beneath my heel. The scent of cinnamon and apple.

The feel of the sand beneath my toes. The rush of the ocean waves. The most ideal white noise to drown out everything.

Those tender, quiet, early morning hours — raw and vulnerable. When the day yawns and wakes, but hasn't quite pulled on its armor yet. And neither have I.

The sound of summer storms and nowhere to be.

That suspension of time where an ending is imminent, but I'm grasping for every last straw before it slips away. Adamantly fighting for just a little longer.

Stars twinkling. A reminder that I am just a speck of dust in this vast, unknown Universe.

Feeling a connection greater than us because some things just... **are**.

Salt in wounds that never seem to close.

Small talk. The kind that delays an inevitable bomb I know is coming.

A full moon with the unwavering audacity to brighten the darkest hours. A reminder that we, too, can still shine in darkness.

Deep belly laughs bubbling up from inside me.

Park benches in the sunshine on warm*(ish)* winter days.

Secret emoji codes.

Mid-kiss giggles for reasons neither of us know.

Words. Strung together in such a way that I'm unable to form my own.

Music that instantly transports me to a specific time, place, and *feeling*.

Joy. Hope. Validation. Fear. Yearning. Disappointment. Ache. Change. You.

BLACK AND WHITE

Most of us
desperately wish for
those answers that are
clear cut,
firm,
straight lines drawn in the sand.
We so often crave
the certainty,
the confirmation
that comes from
an unmistakable
yes or no,
in or out,
this or that.
We look for that
non-negotiable sign,
a definitive way to discern
what is truly best for us.

The problem is, the default is to operate in a framework of *either/or,*
when it's most often, more appropriately, a reality of *both/and.*

Because rarely are things that simple.
Rarely is it one or the other.
Rarely is it black and white.

See, in this game we play,
the rules are ever-changing.
They're arbitrary notions,
just our personal assumptions about right and wrong.
Arbitrary or not, they pin us down.
A nagging tug that ceaselessly pulls in the background,
keeping us tethered to our own
artificially constructed roadblocks.
Trapping us in a perpetual purgatory of gray.

EBB AND FLOW

There is no going back to before,
despite how much promise
that far-fetched notion holds.
Remnants of peace,
a mind that knows quiet,
restful nights that bring nothing but sleep —
such small yet significant gifts
taken for granted.
Those little things,
punctuated by
the quietly ticking hands of time,
feel like far off memories,
like distant reminders of an existence out of reach.

Even though I know to expect the ebb and flow,
as with all things on this Universal stage,
it doesn't make it any easier.
Dancing to a cosmic cadence,
caught in a web of rhythm and blues,
it's all so heartbreakingly beautiful,
this harmony that haunts.

I don't always know the words,
but I trust
the melody of this music
to guide me.
So, I sway with the ebb,
try to go with the flow,
take a deep breath,
rub my bloodshot,
sleep-deprived eyes,
splash water on my face,
and get lost in the tune of today.

WINDED

It grabs at me,
latching on to every last inch of my being.
It wraps me up in its gnarled grasp.

Constantly attempting to evade
its grip,
            I run.

Fast at first,
but my pace inevitably slows.

Whether it's by chance or choice,
I can't be sure.
I'll never be sure.

But I know that
with this extra weight
bogging me down,
I can't keep running anymore.

INVISIBLE INCISIONS

We all go about our lives with invisible incisions.
Some are mere surface level slices —
nothing a Band-Aid and a dab of Neosporin can't fix.

But others cut deep, blade to bone,
like words and memories that **echo**, *hover, haunt,* **sting** —
a brutal antiseptic burn on a perpetually raw wound.

Because though invisible to the outside observer,
these ones never seem to scab over,
their presence unmistakably unrelenting from the inside.

And no matter how much time passes,
no matter how perfect things look from afar,
when we reach down and run our fingers along
these familiar vulnerable spaces,
we always come away with drops of fresh blood.

An ever-present reminder.
A gaping gash.
Not seen, but felt.
Always felt.

NIGHTMARES

I've been waking up from nightmares lately,
and I can't tell if that's a metaphor for something,
or if I'm just reading too much into things, like I do.
It's just,
the night,
with its calm and its dark and its inherent vulnerability,
seems like the perfect opportunity to be preyed upon
by the things that are **too harsh** to view in the glaring daylight.
So sometimes, at 3 am,
when I'm jolted back to reality,
I can't help but
wonder what it all ~~means~~ meant.

IN BETWEEN BEFORE AND AFTER

Open yourself to *this moment.*
Step out of the trappings of *before.*
Untangle from fears of *after.*
Be here.
Right now.
Be still.
Just breathe.

Descend from the
clouds of your mind,
and bask in the meadow
of this experience,
of *your* experience.
Embrace it for what it is —
any and all expectations
cast aside.

Know that you can
deal with tomorrow
when it dawns,
but right now is
the only thing you have,
and the only thing you need
to do
is be
here.

DAYDREAMS

Sometimes the gravitational pull
isn't enough
to keep us grounded here.
An alternate reality
vies for our attention
and wins.
Every time.
Cue the moon and stars,
forget planes and trains and cars
because we don't need them.
We've already arrived.
In this place
where the background blurs
and nothing else that occurs
matters more than this hazy fantasy land
of imagination and possibility.
We're here.
For now.

SITTING DOWN WITH ICARUS

If we sat down with Icarus, what do you think he'd tell us?
Despite the costs, would he urge us to follow in his footsteps,
to fly higher and higher,
enthralled with the ability to take flight,
boldly and recklessly abandoning all sense of caution?

Or would he heed his father's advice and encourage us to do the same?
Would he advise us to keep a safe distance
from the things that shine the brightest,
to ignore the burning itch of twitching wings,
to silence the inner whispers of, "*There's more*"?
Would he have us settling for never being brave enough to find out?

And never mind him, what would we say back?
Would we nod vigorously and say, "*We get it, we get it!*
Wings were meant to fly, and by all means,
we want to experience the full extent of it!"
Or would we play it safe,
pretend we don't feel the things we do,
bury it all deep where we can't hear its screaming,
and insist that we must do what we're expected to?

SALTY AND SWEET

It's salty and sweet,
the way summer sneaks in and
delivers a signature scent,
its accompanying flavor
so specific that with one taste,
it's unmistakable.
A perfect concoction of
time-distorted memory and
sepia shades of nostalgia,
blended with
the technicolor delights
of our tentative tomorrows.
All of this,
paired with
a simultaneous urgency
to safeguard the delicate present
that whimsically pirouettes in the palm of our hands —
with the hope of protecting it from
unforeseen torrents of emotion and
the bitter sting of eclipsed destiny.

GOLD RUSH

It's been what feels like an eternity
since spring { cracked me open }
and then summer finished me off,
ripped / me / in / two,
insides *m e l t i n g* everywhere.

It hasn't been long
since autumn came knocking,
trying *(and failing)* to [push out the heat],
sprinkling tiny deaths behind every corner.

It won't be long
before winter rushes in —
ushering **icy blasts,**
memories of Decembers and Januarys before —
a lifetime ago,
an entire world away.
Back when it was all
gold rush,
   red flush,
      couldn't
        get
          enough.

OSCILLATION

The salt water springs loose,
arrives on its own schedule,
making yet another appearance
before the night comes to a close.
Chaotic in its timing, yet reliable as ever,
it's one steady thing she can count on
as she wobbles through this unsteady season.
Early morning storms,
midday rushes,
a prerequisite for sleep,
no discrimination against time or place.
It's a force that never fails to deliver,
contrary to her wishes.

But when it comes,
cloaked in quiet,
cocooned in the blackness,
it's a flood that carries her off,
drifts her away from this place
and the heaviness saturated with silence.
It's a welcome departure from this oppressive drought.

The irony though, is not lost on her —
this *drought to flood - flood to drought* oscillation.

And as she floats into lucid dreams,
she's vividly aware of how strange it feels
to move so quickly between these extremes.

UNRAVELED

Heaped on the floor, miles and miles of unraveled thread surrounds her /
Her best party dress, once spectacular, is now a drooping tent of fabric / A
yellowed strap slides down her arm / Heavy hair cascades down her back,
a blanket that covers her trembling shoulders, serving as one of the few
constants that grounds her / The crooked and flickering chandelier winks
at her teasingly — simultaneously breathtaking and a mess / Relatable.

She grasps for heaping handfuls of this unruly thread, fastidiously trying
to tease out some pattern, only to find endless knots and dead ends / She's
never one to give up, but she throws her hands in the air / Slumped in
bewilderment, her eyes glisten with emotion, cheeks dampened from the
fallout / Silently, she wishes some fairy godmother would come guide her.

As she is now, tangled in this woolen mess, she's unsure what the best
approach would be / Collect the loose ends and put everything neatly
back together / or leave herself and everything around her unraveled?

SOME THINGS

Some things make us come *alive*.
They peel back our outer shells
and expose the dormant layers we forgot even existed.
They remind us how complex and dynamic we actually are.
They awaken the intricacies of our humanity that too easily get buried
underneath the day to day, the hustle and bustle, the distractions.

Some things *thrive* in the pause.
In the calm, in the quiet,
they find the courage to tap at the doors of our souls
and remind us, *Hey, I'm here.*
They linger when and where they feel safe,
opening up to golden opportunities to shine,
knowing they'll likely be forced back into hiding eventually,
so they should dance while they can, and *dance they do.*

Some things insist on being *felt*,
despite how much more convenient life would be
if they minded their own business,
kept to the shadows,
out of sight, out of mind.
But instead, they come steamrolling in,
bold in character,
asserting their dominance over our plans,
and if nothing else, remind us that
our perceptions of order and control are illusory.

Some things come around to *teach* us.
They deliver lessons that stick with us,
leaving muddy footprints on the floor,
reminding us that sometimes
when we let go of expectations,
we'll find beauty in the mess.

BEGINNINGS AND ENDINGS

Beginnings. Enchanting, exciting, exhilarating. Blinded by promise and possibility. A buoyancy runs like a thread through our day to day existence, making even the mundane glow with joy. We're emboldened by the realization that maybe, sometimes, we actually *can* hold on to the things that light us up.

During beginnings, we're often in over our heads,
but the rush is intoxicating and so
we
plunge
deeper
anyway.
Thrust into the action, we don't always fully recognize the novelty of the moment until we're past it. And once we're past it, there is no returning.

Because we all know beginnings are temporary. Beginnings give way to the in between, which has a color all its own. If we're lucky enough, we get to live out this space for a good while. But things don't always play out that way. Life has plans. The wind blows in a different direction. What once boldly bloomed, bursting with aliveness, suddenly disperses without warning, sending petals in a thousand different directions, remnants of what was once whole and beautiful making a mess everywhere, giving way to something entirely different, reminding us that everything is temporary. Time marches on.

And when the endings come, we feel it in different ways. Sometimes it's a quick rip of the Band-Aid. Startling, but it's over just as fast as it began. We're left reeling, with a lingering pain where we once felt protected. Exposed and vulnerable where we once felt safe. Sometimes, though, it's a slower burn. Sometimes we see the writing on the wall for a while, but don't want to face it. In these cases, it's death by a thousand cuts. There isn't one clear explanation to point to. There's just what is. Browning petals littered all around us. An ending.

And time marches on.

THE DIFFICULT THINGS GET EASIER, THEY SAY

The difficult things get easier, they say.
Maybe they do.
Or maybe
that's just what you tell yourself
to make it through the day.

Brew the coffee.
Chop the vegetables.
Clear every last dish in the sink.
Wash, rinse, repeat.
Until it gets easier.
Theoretically.

Go through the motions —
talk, laugh, work, play.
Your best fake smile
lights up the room,
bright enough to convince
even the most discerning eye
that there is nothing but joy
beneath the surface.
Distractions on distractions.
Stay busy.
It gets easier, they say.

A good time.
A stiff drink. Maybe two.
A song that hits just so.
It helps, but it doesn't.
A few quick blinks and a,
"There's something in my eye,"
as your voice catches in your throat
and you swallow the telltale lump.
It's a familiar eight count
you know by heart at this point.

The music continues.

Alone in a crowded room,
while dueling dragons rage within.
No knight in shining armor arrives.
The demons here,
they're solely yours to slay.
No one can take that away.
But the difficult things get easier, they say.

LONG TIME

She looks me dead in the eyes and says,
"I can't believe I still feel this way."
And I watch, heartbroken, as the tears spill over.
I can see the pain in the redness around her eyes.
Can read the hurt buried beneath the smiles
trying to hold it all together.
Can see how the commas around her mouth
seem to say all the things she wants to, but doesn't.
Can sense the underlying sadness there.
Even in the sunshine.
Even when she's laughing.
Even despite all the blessings.
And I know it.
I do.

I want to tell her
that it won't always be like this,
that it won't always hurt,
that it won't always haunt,
that soon she'll forget,
that they say, *"Time heals everything,"*
that they say, *"It gets easier,"*
that *I know* it gets easier.
But I don't.
I don't.
So, I don't.

NOW IT'S NOT

Scorching summer sun beats down on my skin,
a heat so electrifying it gives me goosebumps.

The pier, riddled with trickling watermarks,
quietly reveals the fleeting presence of waves.
The only trace that

       something was here, and now it's not.

And that's just it, isn't it?

The way things come slamming into being,
staining us a different color,
leaving undeniable proof of existence

a reminder —
as if to say,

       something was here, and now it's not.

SOME FEELINGS YOU JUST CAN'T CAPTURE IN WORDS, LIKE

A cold shower after a long, hot run. Eye contact across a crowded room. How you just fit perfectly into that spot on their chest. Discovering a song that completely aligns with your experience. Words effortlessly pouring out of you...important ones. A gentle, loving touch exactly when you need it. An energetic pull stronger than any logic. When your intuition proves to be right...again. When someone reaches out simply to tell you they miss you. When a memory makes you burst out laughing. When a memory makes you collapse into tears. That deep-rooted tug at the thought of how things used to be...knowing you'll never get that back. The loss of someone you love. Reading old journals and feeling the emotions instantly flood your body. Learning to sit with discomfort. That stubborn flicker of hope that you simultaneously love and hate. That quiet inner knowing that you're exactly where you belong. That unsettling yet reassuring reality that nothing lasts forever.

AMONG OTHER THINGS

It's the glow of the morning sunrise
as I make my way down quiet streets,
coffee in hand.
The grounding feeling of feet on pavement —
left, right, left, right —
centers me.
It's an intimate moment
where I let myself be,
before the rest of the world wakes
and I'm expected to do.
In these early morning meditations,
I notice myself brightening with the sky.
This is one thing that makes me feel alive.
Among other things.

It's the moments of connection
when hearts open
and out pours everything
I never knew I needed to share
with another.
I'm not quite sure why
I say the things,
but I do.
It's as if we reached inside
and touched one another's souls.
Speak first, think later.
Be known.
It's rare.
It's magical.
And when it happens, I *feel* it.
A Universal offering,
sparklers lit from stars,
like, *"Here, you and you, let's make some sparks fly, shall we?"*
It turns the lights on within.
This is one thing that makes me feel alive.
Among other things.

It's the welcoming embrace
of those almost summer nights.
The gentle rustling of trees,
a warm breeze,
the air with an auspicious feel to it
seems to envelope me,
a hug so perfect
I didn't know what I was missing until it arrived.
Feelings —
serenity, joy, contentment, connection with something greater —
abound.
This is one thing that makes me feel alive.
Among other things.

It's also those moments when
I can't ignore the ache in my chest.
The kind that feels like
it will undoubtedly split me in two,
the soul-crushing kind.
I have no choice
but to allow it to exist.
I move with it.
It moves with me.
It moves *through* me,
an unwanted shadow
that I try my best to be hospitable to.
A house guest forever overstaying its welcome.
But I oblige and don't turn it away.
Because this too,
is one thing that makes me remember
that I *am* alive.
Among other things.

CACOPHONY

Not everyone knows this, but
if we take the time
to stop and listen,
we can hear
a chaotic clamor of emotions,
our own and others,
running in the background
at any given moment.
Hear me out.

To start,
there's the light, buoyant
sound of happiness.
It's soft, yet powerful.
Fast and fun.
A bouncy beat,
uplifting and energizing.
It powers us through,
amplifying our experiences
with an auditory dose of sunshine.
Easy listening music.
A preferred tune.

But we wouldn't appreciate
the pleasantry of happiness as much
if we didn't also know
the sound of sadness.
In contrast,
it's deep,
like it's coming from within,
reverberating
low and loud and steady,
a rumble that shakes us to our core,
like it could take us over if we let it.

Then there's the sound of hope.
A warm, gentle, inviting buzzing.
It creates a fuzzy glow,
like a glass of champagne
right to the head.
The pop of the cork,
the bubbles that zip to the top,
we can hear it all
as the optimistic anticipation
springs loose inside us.
And like the first sips of champagne,
the first notes of hope are the best.
But if we're not careful,
if we get carried away,
if we don't keep ourselves in check,
the aftermath can be brutal.

Because hope left unguarded
sometimes gives way to disappointment.
That's not pessimism, that's fact.
And the sound of disappointment
is that of a record abruptly stopping.
An upbeat tempo
suddenly cut off
mid-song,
lips forming the next word
frozen in time,
the line hanging in the air,
the song never finished.
Yet, the tune remains stuck
ringing in our head,
over and over and over,
a maddening repetition,
no matter how many times we sing it.
A constant reminder of what was.
A constant reminder of what wasn't.

Next up is resentment.
Whether we want to acknowledge it or not,
we all know its sound.
We often try to ignore it,
but its telltale bellowing
fades in and out,
despite our best intentions to keep it down.
Really, it's just pain in disguise,
but it's an unmistakable noise.
Familiar, yet foreign.
Full of so many different tones —
bitter and biting,
loving and lamenting,
reeling and regretting,
hoping and hurting,
friction and frustration.
All of these at the same time.
It's a sound of paradox.
It's a sound of complexity.

None of these though,
hit the ears quite like apathy.
This one,
with its jarring absence of
literally everything,
somehow screeches the loudest.
It's earsplitting.
A loaded silence so excruciating
it makes us want to
throw our hands over our ears
and scream.
Quite frankly, it's the
most offensive component
of this godforsaken ensemble.
But it's there.
Oh, it's there,
clearly communicating

detached indifference.
The result?
A relentless ringing in our ears
that fills the emptiness.
A haunting silence that's impossible to silence.

All of these sounds,
among others,
run a constant loop,
always there to some degree or another,
in varying volumes
depending on the time,
depending on the circumstances —
an accompaniment to our existence
whether we choose to fully notice or not.
And when we do tune in
and truly hear them all at once,
it's a dizzying whir we can't escape.
Some might even say
that collectively,
it's too much,
overwhelming,
confusing,
difficult to parse out what's what —
a true cacophony.

WAVES, AGAIN

I've written a lot about the ocean waves,
but it just seems like
they're the perfect metaphor
when there are no other words.
They most accurately capture
the unpredictable rush and retreat
of,
well,
a lot of things.

I keep trying to find something else that
equally conveys what I'm trying to express —
how we're at the mercy of the tides,
an ebb and flow
that is oh-so much bigger than us.
I keep trying to find something else that
has the same effect,
the same *feel* I'm looking for,
but everything falls short,
somehow misses the mark.

So I sit,
stumped,
watching the waves pull back at low tide.
And I'm stuck here,
for now,
toes in the sand,
r e a c h i n g
for something I can't quite grasp.

SHIFTING GEARS

Every so often,
when you least expect it,
you're vividly reminded
just how temporary things are.

Sometimes,
those reminders come brazenly,
an unwelcome form of whiplash
that leaves a lingering tightness
no matter which way you move.
It happens fast,
like going from 0 to 60 to 0
in the blink of an eye.

At first, you're flying,
enraptured by
electricity, joy, novelty.
Your entire body thrums
with a resounding,
yesss thisss.
Cruising full speed ahead,
hair flowing in the wind,
you find yourself joyriding —
it's an enchanting, scenic route
that takes your breath away.
For the time being,
even the impossible
feels possible.

A cool breeze dances along your skin.
The world passes by
in a vibrant array of color.
Every last sensory receptor is
alive, alert, awake.

It's enthralling,
captivating,
so you're not braced for
a drastic momentum shift —
an abrupt stomping on the brakes
without warning.

It's so sudden
as to be bewildering, really.
You're not truly clear on what happened.
All you know for sure is that
the foot, the hard stomp,
wasn't your own.
But you're along on this ride,
so your foot or not,
you feel the impact.

Your body lurches forward,
an automatic attempt to
resist the immediacy of braking.
The seat belt cuts into your skin,
carving what you know
will be a lasting mark.
There's nothing gentle about any of it.
A gear shift this drastic
is a shock to the system,
so jarring
it knocks the wind out of you.

Involuntarily gasping for air,
desperately trying to catch your breath,
your eyes dart to the sky,
in search of
something,
anything,
to help make sense of it all.
But there are just
quiet clouds floating by,

unfazed,
minding their business,
leaving you
to your own devices,
left with no choice but to
resignedly yield
and figure out how
to navigate differently
from here.

WAYS TO SCARE SOMEONE AWAY

after Michelle Awad

Show them who you are. All of you. The light and shadow parts. Let them in on how much you feel. Hold them. Trust them. Fall for them. Hard. Show them how you've scraped your knees *(again)*, and you're a bloody mess *(again)*, but tell them you'll just keep getting up and tripping all over *(again)* because who cares about scraped knees when it feels like this? Show up. With all of you. Thoughts. Feelings. Hopes. Dreams. Desires. Passions. Unapologetically. All your mess and all your masterpiece. Explain that things aren't always black and white, and most often they're gray, and you truly believe the answer box is too small for all the things you feel anyway. Tell them they're *fire* and you're *air* and there's just something *there*. Fly away on paper planes of fantasy. Ask them if they want to come. Ignore the fact that you might erupt in flames mid-flight. Weather the storm through the fog because clear skies do exist and you know it because you've seen them. Be *too much* and *not enough*. Tell them all of it. Show them more. Love them hard. Hand them your heart in a glass jar labeled *Handle with Care* while you're 35,000 feet in the air, and then

watch them drop it.

Note: The line, *"the answer box is too small for all the things you feel anyway,"* was borrowed from a piece titled "How Are We Doing?" by Jess Janz (@jessjanz).

COLLATERAL DAMAGE

I come in,
guns blazing.
Passion, thoughts, feelings
burning me up from the inside,
bursting forth in the form of
unfettered honesty firing from my lips.
I have the best of intentions.
I just want to talk it out.
I just want to find common ground.
I just want to call a ceasefire.
I just want to return to "normal" already.
I just want —

But there's a disconnect,
wires calamitously crossed,
and I feel it all slipping through my fingers
with each passing second.

Inside, I'm unraveling —
emotionally eviscerated
and grasping at straws to keep it together.
Outside,
I'm leaning heavily on this hard outer shell,
this bulletproof jacket,
in an instinctual attempt
to prevent further damage.
But it's all in vain;
my eyes betray me and the tears fall freely.
What good is this armor if it doesn't actually work?

Words rain like bullets out of me,
dissipating in the air.
Remnants dangle in a distant no man's land
instead of landing upon their intended recipient.
Which is, by default,
an effortless counterattack all its own.

In the end,
those words never do land,
but rather ricochet,
hit me while I'm down,
and I'm back where I started.
Hurt again —
collateral damage in the wake of truth.

STORIES

This isn't an earth-shattering revelation:
There's more than one side to every story.

Of course.
We know this.
It's not a new concept.
It's a tale as old as time.
And yet, sometimes
it's hard for us to separate
from the way we saw something
to embrace this grander,
more universal understanding.
Because it's never as simple as,
"This is what happened."
Period. The end.
No.
There is always more to unpack.

The reality is,
everyone has their own account of an experience
that they bring to the table,
but also,
entangled with one's rendition of events
are the joys, hopes, fears, and disappointments
they carried along with it.
This is where the variation is really born —
in the feelings that colored the story being told within.
Each person's inner world humming a slightly different tune.
Each person still acutely aware of how events moved them.
Each person gravitating toward a different way to reconcile
what they felt
with what happened.

It's kind of wild to think
that we move through moments

alongside others,
page after page of story being written,
but really,
we're all just starring in our personal editions of these tales.
We can get so wrapped up in our own narrative
that we sometimes forget we're actually living out
parallel plot lines,
no two stories told the same,
our own experience being the only one we know for sure.

The truth is,
regardless of what we come to understand
about another's interpretation of how things happened,
there isn't one truly objective version of any story.
There isn't one "standard" to turn to,
that we can mark as fact,
title, *"Original Version: True Events,"*
and stack on the shelf with the rest of our life's volumes.
Because it isn't as simple as that.
Because things don't occur in a vacuum.
Because things occur to and between people —
living, breathing, flawed, complex humans.

And we can question the validity
of various perspectives on any given situation,
but ultimately,
valid stories are all the ones we truly *feel* ourselves.
Even if they vary.
Even if the story arcs don't align with another's.
Even if the resolutions don't always come together
the way we thought and hoped they might.
From the very first page,
we're all just authoring
our own personal sagas.
And in the end,
the only stories we really know
are the ones that belong to us.

VULNERABILITY, PRACTICALITY, AND TOOTHPASTE

It seems that there are particular
people, situations, seasons
that inherently evoke the vulnerability within us.
In these cases,
honesty just spews forth,
like toothpaste splattered in
an unconventional work of art
all over the bathroom countertop.
At first, it's liberating
letting every last drop of yourself ooze out.
You beam with joy,
reveling in the authenticity,
taking in the minty masterpiece that ensues.

But no matter how beautiful <u>you</u> think this is,
sometimes,
that zeal is extinguished
when countered with stinging reminders that
toothpaste all over the counter isn't *practical*,
so it's best you clean up after yourself.
>   *Oh.*
>   *Okay.*

Here's where it gets complicated, though.
Because practicality be damned,
sometimes you don't want to clean things up.
Sometimes you like the marvelous mess just fine.
Sometimes, desires aside,
you don't have the first clue
how to go about tidying up anyway.
Because the thing about vulnerability is,
like toothpaste from a tube,
there's no undoing what's already come out.

ON THE BEACH, AT DUSK

Sitting here,
on the beach,
at dusk,
I envy the water.
Certain in its uncertainty.
Fluid and flexible,
yet powerful enough
to move things,
to arrange things
just so,
however it wants them to go.
Filled with treasures
that only those who wade in deep enough
will ever truly know,
save for the scattered bits
and broken pieces
that make their way to shore.

INFORMATION GATHERING

"This is all information," she says
when I'm crumpled on the floor,
a despondent, pondering puddle,
unsure what to make of anything,
most specifically, my current state.
"More will be revealed —
you don't know what's going to happen,"
she further assures me
with a confident, faithful knowing
that makes me pause, chuckle,
and hey, even the tears temporarily abate.
I'll take it.

And I want to believe her.
I want nothing more than
to not only just nod my head in agreement,
but fully, wholeheartedly believe it.
As if it solves everything.
As if it's that simple.
As if it's that easy to just take your hands off the wheel
and trust that you'll get where you're supposed to go,
in a way where you not only *arrive*,
but actually *fall in love with the ride*,
in spite of all of its **roadblocks** and *detours* and breakdowns.
And damn, I want nothing more than for her to be right.

MOON WATCHING

I lie awake and watch the moon
confidently shining through the darkness,
lighting up the sky,
daring us all to sleep on such beauty.

I lie awake and count the headlight flickers
on the ceiling as they pass by.
Each one a missed chance or a dodged bullet —
can't be sure, will never be sure.

I lie awake and watch the minutes tick by,
each one a missed opportunity for peace,
or perhaps just some extra time to think.
I suppose it's a little of both.

I lie awake and think of the others lying awake with me...

The tired, nursing mothers,
desperate for sleep,
torn between wanting to savor these precious moments,
and dying for an exhaustion reprieve.

The heartbroken and grieving,
shattered with ache,
haunted by what was and what could have been.

The quiet lovers
wrapped in each other's arms,
fighting off sleep because right here, right now
is the only place they want to be.

The overthinkers
replaying scenarios in their heads,
wondering if things would be different
if they had only...

The worried souls,
overwhelmed and unsure what to do next.

The restless wonderers,
imaginations running wild, lost in fantasy.

I feel them all.
I wonder if they feel me.
Because things just feel a whole lot more
in these quiet moments,
when you're lying awake,
watching the moon,
while the rest of the world sleeps.

BIG FEELINGS

When I say, big feelings, I mean / how is it actually possible / for me to / feel / this way? / I mean / passion / powerful / burning inside / I mean / not everything / but / certain things / fan the flames / in a way that I can't quite explain / I mean / a song / a note / a line / a word / an overwhelming / swell / within / I mean / a gut punch / I mean / words that aren't enough / but all there is / all I have / I mean / ache / that pulses and throbs / and takes up residence / and insists on staying / no matter how much / I beg it to leave / it refuses to go / **When I say, big feelings, I mean** / feelings so big / so **loud** / so / so / so / that just don't make sense / I mean / knowing that / <u>logic is overrated</u> / and some things / don't / and / won't / compute / <u>ever</u> / and I never liked math anyway / **When I say, big feelings, I mean** / reminding myself of all of that / I mean / riding the waves / I mean / surrendering / **When I say, big feelings, I mean** / pinpricks behind my eyes / before I can draw up the armor / to keep them back / I mean / the lump in my throat / the squeak in my voice / that both come just as fast / **When I say, big feelings, I mean** / feeling like this *feeling* / might just / *wash* / *me* / *away* / I mean / trying to / dig my toes in the sand / as deep as I can / gripping with all my might / fighting / to / stay / grounded / **When I say, big feelings, I mean** / the most terrible / and most magical / gift / yes, gift / bestowed upon me by the gods / like, *"Here, we know it's a lot, but we know you can handle it."*

Because the thing is /

When I say, big feelings, I mean / it's not always **hard** / being this *soft*.

And when / the *sun breaks through the clouds* / and the music picks up / and the *connection* is undeniable / and all I can actually do is / *laugh* and *sing* and *dance* / and feel the electricity / <u>and embrace it all</u> / I wonder / how I could ever / possibly / wish it / wish **I** / was any different.

THINGS NO ONE TELLS US *(but we figure out on our own)*

Logic is overrated.

Hugs are underestimated.

Falling feels like flying.

Contradictory emotions coexist.

Grief is a wild, wild animal. Unruly and untamed.

Time doesn't heal everything. But everyone will tell you it does.

Authentic connection is electrifying.

There is magic in messiness.

Hearts will break a million little (and not so little) times.
And a million times more. *And they'll still have love to give.*

We bend and we bend and we bend and we bend and we —

The Universe knows what it's doing, even if we don't.

Chapters end, but stories never do.

IT'S COMPLICATED

It turns out that my relationship with disappointment is...complicated.

I know most people aren't fond of a letdown / but it seems like / this give and take / I get wrapped up in / is sometimes / heavy-handed / imbalanced / too one-sided / for my sensitive soul to take.

I don't mean to sound naive / I know all too well / that things won't always go my way / and this isn't about that / No / It's more that / the hidden dreamer in me / the idealist that runs rampant through my inner realm / she sometimes feels **possibility** in the most potent sense / She paints dreamscapes of gold and silver / that glimmer in all the right ways / from every possible angle / in every possible light / She gets swept up in the music / in the rhythm / in the glow / Enchanted / Truly / Sigh.

And the silvers and golds and the bright lights of idealism can be blinding / so blinding / that she gets swept away by her unwavering determination / to make things work / to communicate at all costs / to create solutions where the current options don't suffice / Because she feels it / and she wants it / and she knows it / *could be* / But no matter how bright the lights are / sometimes they go out.

Because sometimes **rejection** is all too ready / to *flip the switch* / to **slam the door** / And so / things get complicated / when she dreams it / but it doesn't come / or it does come, but then it *leaves* / **her in the dark** / and then I've got to find ways to / *disentangle* / her from the webs of potential / *maybes* / *had beens* / *would have beens* / that already wove their way into **her** psyche / into her 'reality' / It's trying to separate from something that was / so real (*for her*) / in so many ways / yet never fully saw the light of day.

What more can I say? It turns out, it's... complicated.

IT WAS RARE, I WAS THERE

numb fingertips and warm hearts / it's December and / I can't be sure / if my hands shake / from the electricity of anticipation / or the cold I'm underdressed for / likely both / I've spent weeks waiting on some / elegant epiphany / to hit me over the head / but right now / none of it really matters / does it? / because my moment of revelation comes / when I realize the answers will arrive in time / (and they won't be mine) / but for right now / living in the questions / is the only place to be.

MEMORY LANE

I can't always remember what I talked about at my team meeting three days ago / but it never fails to amaze me how other things have **lodged themselves** into my memory / taken it upon themselves to permanently / take up residence / **refuse to fade** / no matter how much time is put between them.

Like the things you said / and how I _thought_ you meant them.

Or how it felt to fly and then fall / both the **thrill of the flight** / and the **bone-crushing ache** / of the inevitable crash / when you pulled out your parachute / but left me fumbling with mine.

Or the countless hours of conversations / about everything and nothing / details of which / despite it all / I still remember with unmatched precision.

Or that song you learned and played just for me.

Or the feel of your cold hand in mine / a December park bench / goose shit everywhere / an auspicious feel to the sunshine warming the chill in the air.

My navy blue shirt / red lace / black leggings / in a heap on the floor in the dark / The look in your eyes / as I looked up at you / looking at me / propped on your elbow / bodies warm.

The light it brought / and the darkness it left.

The sound of _electricity thrumming_ / **constantly** / in the background.

The abrupt / **gut punch** / of thundering silence / when the power went out.

NOTHING NEW

She always had the inkling that her luster would have an expiration date, but she ignored it. Instead, fell headfirst down the rabbit hole. Fell heart first for all the ways her shine was admired. The way she burned even brighter. The way she felt it to her core. Fell for it all *so hard*. What a sucker.

She always knew that the interest would wane once her novelty wore off. She always feared she was just the sparkle and excitement of something different. She always worried that maybe she wasn't in fact, **somebody**, but just *some* **body**. And she was right. Of course she was.

Because she *knew*. She *did know* deep down that eventually her shiny wheels would be rusted, and it would be her alone, broken down on the side of the road while everything else rolled along. She *did know* that it would be her, cast off, discarded, old news. But she dared to hope. Dared to dream. Dared to believe that it was different. That *she* was different. But it wasn't. She wasn't.

Now, she wakes up in the middle of the night. It's like she can feel time moving. The visions change. But the haunting remains the same. Night after night. It, like her, is nothing new.

NEON STARS AND STICKY TACK MARKS

When they ask about our *undoing*,
let's tell it *how it was.*

Let's call a spade a spade and say
the reality is,
it all meant a lot more to me
than it did to you.
And that I thought otherwise, but I was wrong.
And that I was the fool.

Let's tell them that
I was always thinking out loud,
enveloped beneath our sky of neon stars,
marveling in delight at how they *lit up everything inside,*
searching for constellations
and reveling in the beauty,
even if we were the only ones who could see it.

Let's tell them that
I gleefully reached up to point out the glow,
to highlight how they shone **so bright**
despite the darkness,
that for a minute, your hand rose and met mine,
that for a minute, our fingers interlocked,
that for a minute, *there was lightning.*

Let's tell them that
before I could blink
I watched, stunned,
as you *pulled away,*
as you   pushed   me   away,
    {{ **so hard** }}
            {{ **so fast** }}
I watched *you —*
extending both arms upward,

determined to tear
                    it
                    all
                        down,
                              star by screaming star.

Let's tell them that
I fought,
that *I tried* to stick those magic stars back up,
again and *again* and *again*,
but I could only get so far on my own.
I couldn't reach the ceiling by myself.

Let's tell them that
even self-constructed skies
can be made to feel **real**
if you believe in them,
can be made to be long-lasting
if you want them to.
Let's tell them that *I did.*
Let's tell them that *you didn't.*

Let's tell them that
I boldly dared to dream under that neon sky,
drunk on the possibilities,
living for the hope of it all,
but then one day,
all that remained
was **me**,
glaring sticky tack marks on the walls,
faint remnants of star shapes in the paint,
and fading plastic littered on the ground.

Note: The line, *"When they ask about our undoing"* was borrowed from a piece with the same title by Ana Dee (@ana.dee.writes).

DEMONS

One day fades into the next, and
I watch as you take that box you buried me in
and shove it
deeper and
deeper and
deeper into the back of your closet.
I watch as you pile last season's styles on top,
a growing shrine of discarded things
that once excited you,
that you once donned proudly,
that are now crammed in the back collecting dust —
a heap of ragged nothing on the floor.

I watch as you turn up the music
louder and
louder and
louder —
your makeshift way of drowning out my muffled cries.
Because if _you_ don't hear them they don't exist, right?
Because _your_ experience of things is all it's ever been about.

And the reality is that
you can look away as much as you want to,
you can mute my existence,
you can sing at the top of your lungs,
you can pretend you forget who I am, forget what I was —
go ahead and do it.

But demons are demons, darling.
And yours,
well,
yours all look like me.

SOME DAYS, SOME NIGHTS

Some days are hard,
with the first crack of light
edging its way through the curtains,
tapping on the window
like, *"Come now, it's time."*
Feelings churn in your chest,
savagely threatening to rip you in two.
At times like these,
you're not quite sure
how you'll keep it together another day.
"I can't do this now," you whisper to yourself,
one more last ditch effort,
as futile as all the others.
Because who are you kidding?
You're not really calling the shots here;
you never were.

Some nights are hard,
raw and rough and all too real.
The darkness creeps in,
and you're not quite sure
where your emotions end and the night begins.
It all feels one in the same at this point —
vast,
overwhelming,
endless.

But tomorrow is another day.

DISENFRANCHISED GRIEF

I often wonder how many of us are walking around with disenfranchised grief.
With gaping holes and oozing wounds that refuse to scab over
because our society doesn't allow them
the space needed
to breathe,
to feel,
to ultimately heal.
I'd venture to guess it's all of us.

Because "Land of the Free"
is synonymous with
free of vulnerability, free of making others squirm with our emotional honesty,
free of anything that isn't shiny and fun and "acceptable"
in the confines of a capitalist patriarchy.
Is synonymous with toxic positivity.

It's always,

> *"Be grateful for what you have!"*
> *"Look on the bright side!"*
> *"Oh, it could be a lot worse."*
> *"Hey, cheer up."*
> *"Have you considered medication?"*

And I'm always,

> Has it ever occurred to anyone that humans weren't meant to be
> happy and smile *all* the time? Have they ever considered that being
> a full, complete person entails making space for the melancholy, for
> the sorrow, for the inevitable pain that accompanies being a feeling
> soul in a body that aches sometimes

> because loss and sadness are parts of life?

Because everything we love we'll eventually lose, in some capacity or another.

So have they ever thought that maybe we shouldn't just force a smile because it
makes others more comfortable, but we actually need to allow ourselves to sit
in the darkness for a little, until we eventually find our way back into the light.

UNTITLED

Titles are always the last thing I write.
It just feels premature to make such a bold decision
before knowing how it all goes.
It's like that with us.
I never knew,
never dared to know
where we would end up.
So I never wanted to put a title on our story
because doing so would be a resignation from...
I don't know...
...the magic?
...the wonder?
...the excitement?
...the ability to change course and throw in a plot twist?
Doing so would insinuate that I know how it all comes together.
And I don't.
And maybe I should.
You'd probably think that by now, I do.
But the truth is,
I don't want to.
I'd rather sit here sorting through scribbled lines
and scratched out dreams,
pouring onto the page,
writing and writing and writing,
still unsure what to call it.

ENERGY CLEARING

Once the smoke clears,
when the energy has had a chance to *move*,
there's beauty and wisdom to be found in chaos.
It's an uncomfortably necessary part of it all —
to know that we're living out our soul's purpose,
scrawling lessons into our sketchbooks,
charcoal staining our fingertips,
driven by a deep-rooted desire
to actually learn something new this time around.
All with the goal that
we're not back to this same song and dance
again
in another lifetime.
All with the hope that
our souls have a chance to start fresh in this one.
A clean slate,
a neutral state,
ready to receive what is meant for us.
Whatever that may be.

THE LONG AND WINDING ROAD

Distractions / are good and all / but when everything quiets down / when the vacation is over / when you make it back home / when the party ends / when the guests are all gone / everything is still / right where you left it / **You still have to feel to heal** / You can't "busy" the emotions away / as convenient as that would be / It just / doesn't work like that / And you might think / it's been long enough / *I should be* / *over this by now* / *what is wrong with me?* / And the answer is / nothing / Because again / it doesn't work like that.

Healing / feeling / all of it / there is no timeline / **none of it is linear** / it's always / *one step forward* / and *three steps back* / and days turn into weeks / and weeks turn into months / and you still have questions / with no answers / and at some point / you learn to live with that / not because you want to / but / because you have to / You learn to live *into* the questions / *whatever that means* / you learn to live / with the fact that / you don't have to have it all figured out / and in fact / you never will / and some things / are **always** going to be *the things that remind you of your softness* / and some days / many days / that doesn't feel okay / but it will be okay / because it has to / because there are further chapters to write / and there is a greater wisdom to things / and more will be revealed / and even when that's hard / to sit with / and settle for / it becomes enough / because it has to / and also / it will never be enough / **both of these can be true** / but it has to / it has to / it has to / it has to / it will.

ROSE-COLORED GLASSES

Occasionally,
we have a tendency to look at things —
people, situations, ideas —
through rose-colored glasses.
Everything is shiny, peachy, idealistic
until...it's not.
Until something happens
that violently rips off said spectacles,
reality crushing them under its heel,
leaving us painfully staring into a blinding light
we weren't ready for.
Peculiar patterns dance across our vision,
and suddenly, everything looks *off*.
Suddenly, the entire world just feels *different*.
It's moments like these that make us
wonder if things had always been this way
or if something actually changed.
I suppose we'll never know.
And while I'm not one to shy away
from the the truth of what is,
sometimes,
I can't help but think
certain things sure looked better
with those rose-colored glasses still on.

REVOLVING DOORS

Revolving doors have always made me nervous / Maybe that's silly / but I'm always unsure / of how to approach them / Always afraid I'm going to / time it wrong / misstep / and get stuck / bones crushed between the glass / *halfway in one world, halfway in another* / my pain and my folly / on display / for everyone to see / *Oof.*

It always complicates things further / when I'm not the only one trying to make it through / this maze of an entryway / this kaleidoscope of spinning and glass / this portal to another place / Things get even more complex / when I'm there / side by side / with another.

Do we go together? / *Do we go separately?* / We stand there / awkwardly dancing around each other / both clear on the WHAT / but equally stuck on the HOW / Classic.

For a moment / the goal is mutual: *get through the door.*
But that moment is gone just as quickly as it arrives.

Because if I linger too long / diligently deliberating the best course of action / before I know it / the decision is made without me / no definitive discussion to be had / It just concludes with / *I'm going now, and you can figure out the rest on your own* / punctuated by an unspoken / *Not my problem* / ringing / in the departing breeze.

And before I can even blink / I'm blinking back / at my lonely reflection in the glass / wondering again / how fast or slow I should move / *to get through it* / the "it" now an entirely new type of conundrum.

Eventually / I do find myself / putting one foot in front of the other / or was it that something pushed me forward? / Unclear / Either way / all I know is that / next thing / I'm moving / and then *everything is spinning* / and I'm just hoping / I come out on the other side / *intact* / someone I'd still recognize / if I saw her staring back at me.

So, when I inevitably find myself / back at these revolving doors / both the thrill / and the wariness / growing / screaming / I think surely, I'll get it right this time.

But the timing is off / <u>again</u> / And this time / instead of being left / standing alone / staring at my reflection / I'm slammed face first into the glass / and that's when I realize / I had it all wrong.

That's when I realize / it wasn't actually about the timing / *ever*.

It was about *trusting*.
It was about *knowing*.
It was about *sensing*
when to push forward / and when to pull back / Because if you don't read that right / before you know it / before your eyes / <u>someone else will do the pushing and pulling for you</u> / and not necessarily in the direction you want.

Because it turns out / that eventually / even revolving doors / lose steam / break down / give up / and then you're stuck / heart smashed between the glass / *halfway in one world, halfway in another.*

VERTIGO

I've never been an all or nothing person.
Which is fine and good until
all or nothing is thrust upon me,
the rug ripped out from underneath,
the balance I thought I had
immediately trampled
by an unrelenting case of vertigo.
Nothing looks the same.
It's all blurred lines
through blurred eyes,
the scene always shifting,
never quite in focus,
swirling
endlessly.

ROBOTS AND TIME MACHINES

I should have known when you first cried 'robot'
that you'd eventually escape in your time machine and never look back.
I should have known I'd be the one trapped in another world,
choking on exhaust fumes,
dizzied by your blatant disregard for the
damage of your departure.
I should have known when we first skipped town
that eventually you'd be the one to leave,
just as fast as you came.
I should have known that you'd have your way,
pull the plug, and vanish —
leaving me floundering alone in the dark.

INTIMATE STRANGERS

I've never been a fan of goodbyes / I mean, who is, I guess?

I just think / it's one of the saddest things / when people who are / close / become / *strangers* / Because I just think / it's truly remarkable / when two beings / open up / in a way where / they connect on a deeper level / Because what's crazy is that / things had to unfold in such a way / the stars had to align / *just so* / that you and you / found each other / and more specifically / found the invisible *thread of gold* that ties you together / And sometimes it's shared / passions / interests / history / that does it / any or all combinations of them / Or not / To be honest / sometimes it's none of that / Sometimes it just is / inexplicable / It just is / an energetic connection / It just is / a pull.

And when you're pulled into / this container of closeness / you see one another / hold space for one another / *know* one another / All the big and little things that make each tick / But things can change / and close now doesn't mean close forever / and sometimes / *"I just need space"* / becomes / *"I don't have space...for you."*

And this is the part / where I want to look away / Like the scene in the movies / where the killer runs in with the knife / and I throw my hands over my ears / and squeeze my eyes shut / because / I / don't / want / to / see / it / I don't want to sit back and watch as / the final cut comes / I don't want to sit back and watch when / the goodbye comes.

But eyes open or shut / it comes / It pounds at the doors of unwilling hearts / and then barges in without regard for readiness / The closeness crumbles / disintegrates / Souls separate / yet still silently orbit around one another / living life on different planets / And I think <u>that's</u> the ultimate tragedy, I do / This intimate connection / BOOM / to / *complete strangers* / overnight / *Oomph* / There's nothing quite like it / And I can't help / but feel like / it's such an unfortunate waste / of a real / special / thing / but maybe it's just me / who thinks about / things like that.

Like I said / I've never been a fan of goodbyes / I mean, who is, I guess? / But / this kind / just feels like / a certain level / of / rip / your / heart / out / But sometimes I think / maybe it's just me / who cares about / things like that / which is / in and of itself / a certain level / of / **rip** / **your** / **heart** / **out**.

PEOPLE ~~DON'T~~ CHANGE

You always said, *"People don't change,"*
and then went and proved yourself wrong.
Demonstrated with a chest puffed full of bravado
that they most certainly do.

You made it crystal clear that they change —
like how they change their mind,
like in the way spring is actually four seasons in one,
and how you never know which conditions to dress for.
Like how one moment the warm air is bursting with life,
only to be stomped out by a sudden cold the next,
an unwelcome early spring snow with a chill
that lingers.

You made it clear that they change,
like how a thing matters
until it doesn't.
Like how it was something more
until it couldn't be less.

And so, if *people don't change*,
then tell me
what to make of this?

SOUR PATCH

Your empty promises echo
in this unnecessary vacuum of your creation.
Their bitter metallic taste caught in my throat
refuses to go down
no matter how hard I swallow.
It's like my own built-in red flag detector
when I'm too cross-eyed to see straight,
my body's way of calling bullshit
on all the things you said,
which were simply a means to an end in the end.

I rinse my mouth time and time again,
but I can't wash away the sour truth.
That I always said, that I always knew
it would be a *"want what you can't have 'til you have it and don't want it"*
thing for you.
That it would all play out on your terms (*always*).
That there'd be nothing I could do.

EVEN STARS

Did you know that even stars burn out?
You probably did.
Anyway,
it's said that it could take billions of years,
but typically,
the more massive the star,
the more quickly it burns up its fuel supply,
thus the shorter its lifespan.

So it's like saying
the things that shine the brightest,
the biggest,
the most intensely,
the things that glimmer and twinkle
and send their fire through the atmosphere
the strongest
will burn out,
collapse,
explode into a supernova
more quickly than the rest.

It's worth mentioning
that "quickly" in space terms
is actually millions or billions of years,
but still.
It's like they're too good for their own good.
And so it culminates in this
exquisite expiration,
an act of rebellion that underscores the
inescapable impermanence of it all.
How noble.
How bold.

Oh, and also,
did you know
that even stars scream when they die?

Literally.
How heartbreakingly beautiful —
they make their glimmering glory
unmistakably known one final time before
exploding and finally settling into
a black hole,
lost among the ethers,
their visible beauty forgotten,
but their magic forever
        dusted
                across
                        the
                                Universe.

SOFT

I woke up from crying in a dream the other day.
Isn't it wild?
That there are things that move us so deeply,
the waking hours just aren't enough.
They have to creep in under the cover of darkness too,
when we're tricked into thinking
we'll have some semblance of respite from feeling.
Gets me every time.

I could try to say something
profound and deeply metaphorical,
but the simple truth is,
we just can't run from the things that
remind us of our *softness*.

TIME AND TIME AGAIN

I call out
and hear my own voice
e c h o   b a c k   t o   m e
time and time again.
Each one {{ reverberates }}
louder than the last.
And even though
this familiar, one-sided
call and response
is a tired, old song,
a tune I know by heart
like the back of my hand,
the haunting emptiness
still **cuts** me to my core
time and time again.

THE MOMENT I KNEW

I knew I had it all wrong when you spoke over me the second you didn't like what you heard. From the way I couldn't say two sentences without being bulldozed by your objections. In how, despite my assertive pleas, you wouldn't even just *listen*. By the way you threw up defenses and never tried to understand my feelings — just spat condescension at them like they disgusted you, sunk your teeth into my softness, venom oozing from every exposed vulnerability.

I knew I had it all wrong when I saw how adamantly dedicated you were to your own situational pessimism. How you'd been bolstered by your close-minded superiority complex, suddenly empowered by your hard-headed refusal to see any side but your own. In how you assumed the authority to single-handedly make decisions on behalf of all parties involved, and then had the *audacity* to police how I dealt with the fallout.

I knew I had it all wrong when I saw how unwilling you were to face the truth. When you fired off angry rebuttals because you didn't want to admit that what I said might actually be right. I knew I had it all wrong when it clicked that you're too wrapped up in your own ego to redefine status quos and think outside the box. That you're too stubborn to embrace possibilities that aren't black and white, that exist in the gray, that aren't *your* way.

I knew I had it all wrong when your true colors left me blinded. When you ripped off my tinted glasses leaving flickering light spots dancing across my vision. When the picture came clearly into view and showed me a completely different you. When your unexpected ire stopped me dead in my tracks. When hot tears stung my face while your frigid cold froze me in place. When your bitter overpowered any lingering remnants of sweet. When you met my open hands with closed fists.

I knew I had it all wrong when despite everything that came *before*, you being right was your only possible after.

That was the moment I knew.
I couldn't have been more wrong about you.

PIECES

She stood / braced against an endless night / as the fire blazed before her / Shakily / she collected / all her scattered pieces / fingers grazing the jagged edges / the deep grooves / and piercing corners / she'd come to know by heart.

Still sharp as ever / even after all this time / they nicked her skin / drawing blood / <u>again</u> / a final rebellious reminder / of all the pain they'd brought / that they'd continue to bring / if she persisted / in trying to carry them / **alone**.

This is where she faltered / Never one to be a quitter / it felt *unnatural* / **to just give up like that** / It went against everything inside her / But, she'd seen it done / not long ago / a quite effortless execution, really / She might as well follow suit / Nothing left to lose.

So / there she was / feet firmly planted / shoulders back / chin up / she exhaled / and / with all the heart she had left / tossed with two full hands / into the flames.

Tears streaked her face / as she looked on / while those precious pieces caught fire / And she watched / as glimmers grew / into hope rising from the ashes.

HOPE RISING

Hope rising from the smoke
like a phoenix from ashes
beckons a new day,
and with it,
a new us.

PROOF...ISN'T IT?

I exhale and watch my breath
l i n g e r then   *leave.*
At first,
the foggy warmth swirling
takes shape in front of me —
irrefutable proof that it's real.
Isn't it?
I mean,
I see it, and
I feel it, and
I know it, but
when I reach out to touch it,
it evaporates into nothingness,
and it's gone.

THIS IS ME TRYING

after Taylor Swift

This is me **trying** / This is me swallowing my pride / This is me making a fool of myself (*again*) / This is me extending the olive branch (*again*) / This is me setting aside the hurt (*for now*) / This is me knowing (*it will still be there later*) / This is me **trying** / This is me figuring out how to be (*not too hard, not too soft*) / This is me attempting to bury the hatchet / This is me **trying** / This is me wanting to say everything, but resolving to say nothing / (*because / fresh start / clean slate*) / This is me proving faults in the doubt-ridden "practicality" / This is me **trying** / This is me embracing the mess / This is me giving it my best / This is me **trying** / This is me pretending *I'm fine* / This is me taking what I can get / This is me navigating this grief / This is me ~~coping~~ "*making peace*" with the rest / This is me **trying** / This is me forever wondering / (*did I make it up?*) / (*was it real?*) / (*did any of it matter?*) / This is me examining artifacts that ~~prove~~ proved existence / This is me knowing that energy doesn't lie / This is me **trying** / This is me still holding tight to scattered broken pieces / This is me cutting my hands *again* and *again* and *again* / This is me bleeding through bandages / This is me **trying** / This is me forcing the forgetting of everything ~~that was~~ / This is me throwing away the map / This is me questioning ~~who~~ *what* I was (*to you*) / This is me becoming who I am now (*who is she?*) / This is me **trying**.

DAYLIGHT SAVING

we   spring   forward

      and

    I

  fall

back

into // flashbacks //
of this time
in a different time

because memories aren't [bound] by
the numbers on the clock or the calendar,
but rather they're ((wrapped up))
in the breezes that *roll in* with the seasons —
in the way hearts {{ flutter }} with the *winds of possibility*
in the way the day **holds out** against the night
in the hope that the warmth will *bend* to our will

in the way I ~~believed in it all~~
        was a fool for it all <u>then</u>

in the way I can feel it all <u>still</u>

SEVEN MINUTES, FOUR SECONDS BEFORE THE METEOR HITS

after Amy Kay

We're languorously lounging, legs intertwined, two forms as one melted into the couch. I suggest, for once, that we should split the last strawberry instead of you generously letting me have it like you always do because I only find it fair that both our taste buds should know such simple pleasures in the end. I refill our champagne glasses, yet again, because who cares about champagne hangovers when the world is about to end? You play that song for me one more time and my eyes fill in an instant, right on cue, and you give me that look you always make when you play and my emotions take over and I inevitably cry — somewhere between, *Are you serious?* and *I find it endearing just how much you feel.* And feel I do — all of it, all the time, but especially now as the time is ticking down.

I glance out the window and see the start of what I know will be the most breathtaking cotton candy sky, and I grab your hand, guitar pick and all, and full force pull you out the door because you know I'm not going to erupt into flames without being swept away by one final sunset. I think of all the times I felt alive — always when I was dancing and there was music and magic and kissing and laughter and I want all of it, right here, right now. But we're outside now, so the music has stopped — but it never really stops, does it? And at this point, fuck it all, right? Who cares what the neighbors think? Who cares what anyone thinks? And that's when I realize there **IS** music if you train your ears to hear it. And the next thing I know, I'm dancing, arms in the air, head thrown back, twirling on my highest tiptoes one last time right there in the driveway because there's no time to waste on anything but the things that make my heart soar. And I'm spinning and spinning and spinning and spinning and looking at you looking at me as if I've lost my goddamn mind, and that's when I see a flash, and I hear a scream, and your expression changes, and I reach for you, and it——

hits.

WHEN IT ENDS

When it ends / I hope I'll be able to look back fondly / with lips that curve up rather than down / with eyes that remain dry / with my heart fully intact / I hope to let the warmth wash over me / and feel a fuzzy glow / not the pain of flames / tearing me apart from the inside out.

When it ends / I hope I'll remember the joy for what it was / true elation / possibilities / the vibrancy of life / an actual snapshot of how it feels to be alive / the essence of the human experience / I'll see a bittersweet chapter that was over before it started / one I tried to keep writing / but whose pages turned to dust in my hands / So I'll sit with unclenched fists / arms out / palms open / fingertips coated with celestial sparkles and nostalgia / and *I hope* / I'll know peace / *at last.*

When it ends / I hope I can say I'm better for it / I hope I can look around me at all the layers I painstakingly peeled back and examined / the ones I boldly owned / the ones that were liberating to shed / the ones that reared their ugly heads in resistance over and over and over / the ones I watched bloom and then shrivel and eventually crumble into nothingness / inevitably taking parts of me with them.

When it ends / I hope I'll stand in awe looking at the walls I built back / brick by solid brick / with aching hands and a humbled heart / marveling at the time it took / at how deeply my foundation shook / at how I thought getting there would surely kill me / but it didn't / **it didn't...**

When it ends / when it ends / when it ends / I'll be ready.

VULNERABILITY SOUNDS LIKE

Can we talk? I have a lot on my mind. I'm scared. I don't want it to be this way. I want to say how I feel, but I'm scared it will mess things up. I care about you. I miss you. I miss that. I miss then. Do you miss me? Actually, don't answer that. I feel like I can trust you. I can't believe I'm telling you this. I don't know why I told you that. That made me really happy. YOU make me really happy. This makes me anxious. I'm deeply disappointed. That hurt me. So much. I thought I meant more. I made a mistake. I was wrong. That was my fault. Your entire energy changed; I feel it. I know when you're ignoring me; I can feel that too. I thought it would be different. I hoped it would be different. I thought you were different. *My gosh*, this is painful. When will it ever not be painful? I feel stupid for caring so much, but I just do. Hey, why don't we just be friends already? Would you keep me company? Can I just...have a hug? I don't know how this will go, but I'm willing to try. I had a dream about you. Again. This is difficult. I don't know what to do. I barely ever go a day without crying. What if this never goes away? What if things never change? I don't know if I trust my own intentions. I don't know what to do with my life. The other day I thought of that time when we randomly fell into a fit of giggles and it made me smile. How are you, *really*? You can tell me. What keeps you up at night? Are you scared? What do you *actually* want? I'm overwhelmed by all the things I feel sometimes. Some days are so hard. *Why* is this so hard? Sometimes I wish I could escape to a fantasy world. Would you want to come with me? I wish things were different. Things *were* different. Things *are* different. I hate it. This feels impossible. I have no idea how you're going to take this. This is me trying. I'm sorry. I love you.

TODAY WE SHOULD NOT CRY

Today we should not cry simply because the sun is shining. The sun is shining and the birds are chirping, and it seems offensive to feel this much in conditions like this. In conditions like this, everyone is buzzing and expects you to vibrate at a high frequency too. To vibrate at a high frequency too, obviously you can't be bothered with tears. You can't be bothered with tears because no one wants to see that. No one wants to see that because in a society like ours, *feeling things* is deemed a finite experience, and at a certain point, people determine it's enough. At a certain point people determine it's enough, and you wonder when "people" became the authority on your experience. "People" became the authority on your experience when someone, definitely a straight white man, decided that strength means hiding how we really feel. Hiding how we really feel is just one of the many ways we're taught to go through the motions of this so-called "life" because we're told *it's easier that way, it's simpler that way, it has to be that way. It's easier that way, it's simpler that way, it has to be that way* has to be one of the biggest loads of bullshit humans condition themselves to believe. Humans condition themselves to believe a lot of silly things though, in my honest opinion, but topping that list is that today we should not cry simply because the sun is shining.

EACH DAY BEGINS WITH

rose-colored daydreams and half-hearted hopes
that somehow snuck their way through another night

affirmations whispered to the ethers
alongside solemnly resigned surrenders

hearts caught on barbed wire —
impossible to go forward or back without bleeding in one spot or another

recognition that we still don't have all the answers —
that more will always be revealed

the sun splashing promise across the sky —
a reminder that when the Universe talks, we should listen

NEVER THE SAME LOVE TWICE

"There are all kinds of love in this world, but never the same love twice." - F. Scott Fitzgerald

Like the love born of 5-year-old bedtime snuggles and TCBY frozen yogurt. The kind where mom and dad were flawless superheroes. The kind molded by innocence and youth. The kind of love marked by a childish naivety you never get back.

Like the love born of 13 and 14 and 15 and 16. The first real romantic kind. The kind born of high school football games and basement parties. The kind fuzzied by Captain Morgan in red Solo cups. Stolen kisses in your family living room. A banana split at the beach with spoons for two. The kind where they sneak over and toss rocks at your bedroom window while you're sprawled on your bed reading. Where you trudge over, pull your curtains back, and stare incredulously, real time recognizing how this movie moment is actually your own life.

Like the love born of 17 and 18, passionate and new. The kind of checking your phone in the middle of the night and falling asleep to romantic fantasies. Of sleeping on floors and never being happier. Of being swallowed in a serotonin sea. The kind of love you felt all over as the wind swept over you, the windows down driving, music so sweet type. The kind of love where Mom sighs and says, "I just want you to be happy."

Like the love born of 19 and 24 and 28 and 31. Each one a vignette all its own. Both the forbidden kind and the staying kind. And most importantly, the self kind. The love that lingers and defies all odds and most especially, your wishes. The kind of love that does what it wants regardless of what you want. The quiet love and the loud love. The love that grows and deepens and evolves and redefines what love is. Day after day. Month after month. Year after year. The love that shows you just how deeply you can feel. The love that breaks your heart and the love that holds you together. The love that tucks you in at night. The love you wake up for in the morning.

The kinds of love that stay with you. And they all do. In their own way. The truth is, we'll know so many loves in this lifetime, we will.

But never the same love twice.

I USED TO BE A GIRL

I used to be a girl who believed in fairy tale endings and happily ever afters. Who believed in a life with road maps and clear-cut answers. Who didn't know who she'd become, but who always knew who she was. Who believed she'd have cracked the code of life by thirty because thirty somethings definitely had it all together.

I used to be a girl who saw her worth the way society taught her to. Who cared a great deal about what people thought of her. Who tried to check every box and fit every mold. Who swallowed conflict with her daily vitamins. Who fought constant battles with the expectations in her head, an undoubtedly combustible mixture of both internal and external pressures. I used to be a girl who was scared to take up space. Who hadn't yet learned that humans weren't meant to fit into boxes.

I used to be a girl who thought life was about coloring inside the lines. Who didn't know it's supposed to get messy. I used to be a girl who kept parts of herself closed. Who shied away from the vulnerability of being known. Who hadn't yet learned that staying open is what makes life worth living. I used to be a girl who didn't speak up for what she wanted. Who kept quiet to keep the peace because she didn't want to be "difficult." Who suffered quietly at the mercy of her feelings because feelings made her "dramatic." I used to be a girl who hadn't yet learned that feeling is a superpower. That feeling is courage. That softness is strength. I used to be a girl who hadn't yet learned that she'd much rather embrace softness than be a robot.

I used to be a girl who assumed linearity. Who falsely presumed that growth, healing, change, and letting go all moved in a straight line. I used to be a girl who thought that life and love were black and white. Who didn't know that actually, everything exists in the nuances. In the, *some of this and also that.* I used to be a girl who thought she'd eventually find a way for it all. Who hadn't yet learned that the realist trumps the hopeless romantic every time.

I used to be a girl who didn't know that hope is a double-edged sword. Who believed that people would surely care if they saw how much it mattered. I used to be a girl who thought she could always change things if she worked hard enough. Who hadn't yet learned that in some cases, there's only so much she can do on her own. Who hadn't yet seen that sometimes it's just not as important to others as it is to her. I used to be a girl who thought that hurt was finite, and that pain would stop when she wanted it to. I used to be a girl you wanted to know. I used to be a girl who knew you.

I used to be so many things that I am no longer.
I used to be.
I used to be.
I used to be.
A girl.

Note: The line, "*the realist trumps the hopeless romantic every time*" was borrowed from a piece titled "The Olive Theory" by Eliza (@poetry.by.eliza).

ALWAYS ROOM

She's here again, and she's stronger than before / This time, she's determined / to shake the cobwebs from her aching bones / to dust off the residual heartache / to release all the pent-up pain lodged inside her / This time, it's time for her / to break free from the shackles / to carve out new memories / new feelings / new joy.

And yes, here, even here, especially here / in the same place that broke her / Yes, here / where her **body keeps the score** / where it all comes rushing back *every* time / where her insides are thrust into full on rebellion / stomach churning / eyes burning / heartbeat forgetting its natural rhythm / muscle memory so visceral / it **somersaults her soul.**

But yes, here, even here, especially here / she can find new peace / new comfort / She can dream of more / so much more / Because that's the thing about being human / **the breaking is infinite, but so is the love that puts us back together** / And there's always room for more love / there's always room / there's always room.

IMPRINTS ON THE SOUL LOOK LIKE/FEEL LIKE/SOUND LIKE

hands laced under sunny skies — one small, one large — calloused fingers gently tracing along the curve of knuckles / a cotton candy sunset that arrives just when you need it most / lifetime upon lifetime of hide and seek / rendezvous / deep conversations / people who just get it / get you / remembering the details / the right hug from the right person at the right time / the opening notes of certain songs strummed on the guitar — an instant energetic flood / fingertips reaching, reaching, reaching — just missing, always missing / being relegated from something to nothing / trash to treasure, treasure to trash / the cold, metallic slice of scissors / bleeding / turned backs punctuated by slamming doors / being the thing left on the cutting room floor / the bitter sting of being blatantly and deliberately ignored / your heart in a glass jar, in once trusted hands, dropped from 35,000 feet in the air / shattering / silence / silence / silence / silence / trying and trying and trying and trying and knowing full well it won't make one ounce of difference / silence / misplaced hope / winless fights / rejection / you as the only one who gives a damn / silence / silence / silence.

TIPS, STRATEGIES, AND OTHER IDEAS THAT WON'T WORK

My therapist and I discuss
how I can focus on where to pour my love
in the moments when I'm feeling sad about the other things.
I spin a ring around on my clammy finger,
nod affirmingly,
say it sounds like a great plan,
act like it's some novel idea,
act like I'm not already one step ahead of her.

What I don't say is that I actually know this.
I've been trying to do it for ages now.
It sounds simple in theory,
feels harder in practice,
but I look at you and how you've managed
to erase all traces of caring,
and I wonder if you'd throw me a tip or two,
if it would even make a difference if you did.

But it doesn't matter.
Because I know you won't.
And I know it wouldn't.
So, I just keep trying on my own.
Nodding my head, opening my heart,
pouring and pouring and pouring.

DELICATE

I navigate the day with a lump in my throat
and the stinging behind my eyes.
You know the kind.
The kind where any little thing —
a fork jammed in the kitchen drawer,
a kneecap smashed on the table edge,
an endlessly unyielding silence,
a certain line or a certain song or a certain flashback
just rips open the floodgates, and
any shred of composure I had been white-knuckle gripping
gets *washed away*,
swept up in the current,
dragged downstream,
until eventually,
I, too, wash up on shore,
just a delicate shell,
for the time being,
in need of a soft place to land.

EXPANSION

cross-legged on the floor
clementine peels and pistachio shells
scrawled lines on notebook paper
whiskey neat and
a stack of books by the window
crescent moon peeking in
a little melody strummed on the guitar
intermittent laughter floating through the room
I expand with it all —
these words
this tune
our sound
my heart

LITTLE BIG MOMENTS

I abandoned all expectations a while ago.

But that doesn't mean I'm immune
to the way the dawn bends and breaks across the sky,
painting the horizon in brush strokes of
tangerine, ochre, and rose gold.

It doesn't mean I'm immune
to the chill in the air that
shamelessly lingers on my skin,
that makes me pull my sweater tight.

These little big moments
that stop me in my tracks,
steal my breath away,
send shivers down my spine.
They carry me away
from this place and time,
and I find myself somewhere else,
again,
no expectations,
just feeling —
alive.

LOVE IS

Love is, *Sure, I'll come with you.* Love is, *I heard this song and it made me think of you.* Love is constant voice messages back and forth with your best friend. Love is, *I just wanted to say hi.* Love is, *I miss you.* Love is, *Do you need anything from the store?* Love is, *I took this picture of the sky because I knew you'd love it.* Love is, *You have to do what's best for you.* Love is, *We'll find a way to make this work.* Love is, *Hey, we're in this together.* Love is, *How can I support you?* Love is the first thing you think about when you wake up in the morning. Love is the last thing that floats through your mind when your head finds the pillow each night. Love is the song that just hits — right how you need it to. Love is, *I did that so I could hear you laugh.* Love is, *I figured you'd want this, so I got it for you.* Love is knowing all their routines and quirks by heart. Love is muscle memory. Love is hurt that lasts too damn long because you just care *that damn much.* Love is, *I'm doing this because I know it will make you happy.* Love is, *Do you want to talk about it?* Love is, *I wanted to make you smile.* Love is the beauty of magical beginnings. Love is the ache of unwanted endings. Love is, *How can I help?* Love is, *I'm not going to give up on you.*

Love is all the delicate and tender things.
Love is everything solid and dependable.
Love is you.
Love is me.
Love is.
Love is.
Love is.

LIMINAL SPACES

Sometime I feel like I exist
more in the liminal spaces
than anywhere else.
More in that in between world,
not quite here,
but never quite there —
no,
never there,
never there.
And try as I might
to convince myself
to let it be,
to not care,
the truth is,
I do,
I do,
I do.

LESSONS FROM LEAVES

With envy,
I watch the trees
dive headfirst into this new season,
eager to shed the versions of a time long gone.
It's gradual, the progression
from a vibrant canopy of green, bursting with life,
to a blazing fire that engulfs everything in sight,
to an eventual settling
into brown dried up remnants of what was,
silent, but for the inevitable crunch,
the familiar snap underfoot
as we try to move along.

These reminders,
scattered everywhere,
encourage us to go ahead and
live boldly,
change colors,
lose ourselves in the free fall,
and then carry on —
as readily as the seasons do —
as if it's just that simple.

MORNING REMINDERS

I've come to the conclusion that I have a thing for sunrises.

Maybe it's the quiet strength, the calm confidence,
with which it draws the day out of its shell.

Or maybe it's the effortless simplicity that is both
extraordinary and commonplace at the same time.

Or perhaps it's the unassuming brilliance with which it radiates
like, *"I know I'm magnificent, I don't need to be loud."*

But really there's just something reassuring
in the knowledge that even if
there are parts of yesterday that have slipped from our grasp —
(other beautiful things like
small moments, new beginnings,
watercolor dreams, to name a few) —
a new day brings with it a promise
that there will be more to come,
even if the colors are different.

And I guess it's also that the sunrise,
unlike most things,
is a **constant** we can count on arriving again and again,
even though we'll never get the same one twice.

It's a daily reminder that
yesterday's magic won't return to us,
no matter how long we wait for it,
but there will always be more beautiful things
if only we stop,
open our eyes,
and truly _see_ them.

And maybe that's the real power I'm drawn to.

HEALING IS A RHYTHM

Healing is a rhythm —
one step forward, three steps back.
A continuous *contract and release* of
love in slow motion,
sunset lies,
vertigo dreams —
all crescendoing into a comfortable grief draped in blue,
that last guest at the party
who keeps promising to leave after, *"Just one more song."*

NOTES ON SURRENDERING

I surrender to the will of the Universe
because as it is, I have no cards left.
I've showed my hand,
bared my soul,
pulled out all the stops in my bag of tricks,
to no avail.

And at some point,
when you're the only one trying,
when you've given it all the effort you can,
when you've laid out every possible permutation
and it's still met with thundering rejection,
you just have to know when to give up,
when to give in,
when to accept that
no matter what you do,
you can't change things on your own.

Heart on your sleeve be damned,
you just have to know
when to raise the white flag,
when to throw in the towel,
despite how incongruent it feels in your bones,
despite all the resistance that you know.
You just have to.
Despite.
Despite.
Despite.

STRANGERS, DATES, AND OTHER WEIRD THINGS
ABOUT LIVING A LIFE

It's crazy to think we're all just / a bag of bones / on a rock / hurtling through space.

And because of that / it seems so pointless / how much my body and brain involuntarily hold on to dates and memories / like it's actually going to serve some productive purpose in the end / Spoiler alert: it doesn't.

It's just crazy to me / how you can look at your Instagram story archive and see what you shared on this day last year / and in an instant, you're transported / you remember exactly what you were thinking / feeling / doing / hoping to do / and how some days were *so good* / and others were *so hard* / and isn't it crazy how there are only so many days that exist?

So like, when a specific day rolls around the next time / (*because every day has happened before*) / you think about what you did on that day in a previous time / in a completely other time / and that's just it / it's the same day / but it's literally a lifetime away / And now that day just becomes a point in time / just something that happened to you once / but that isn't within reach anymore / just a blip on the radar of things that have occurred in your life / and then gone / And people say you only get one life / but how can you live so many different lifetimes in it?

And I find that sometimes dates are nothing but reminders / of fleeting moments / of people you spent a finite amount of your precious existence with / to whom you spilled your deepest secrets / to whom you divulged your biggest insecurities / shared your wildest dreams / had your highest highs / and lowest lows / only to find that you don't even talk to each other anymore / don't even know each other anymore / That just seems so wild to me / to deeply know someone and then not / what a bizarre and heartbreaking reality to face / But nonetheless / they left their timestamp on your life because of this date / Because at one point in time / you did that thing / with that person / on that day / and felt that way / even if now you're strangers / even *though* now you're strangers / even if **you** *don't want to be* strangers.

It's just all so strange / and I wonder if / when certain days roll around / and you remember what you did / and what you said / I wonder if those people you did them with / and said them to / I wonder if they remember too / wonder if they think about it too / if they think about you too.

Like I've said / it's crazy to think we're all just / a bag of bones / on a rock / hurtling through space / We're all just these transient characters in one another's stories / and we're the only ones who *really know* the narrative / the most unreliable of narrators, for sure / But the only ones who *really know* the underlying themes / who *really know* the conflicts that **scream the loudest** / we're the only ones who know / we're the only ones who know / *we're the only ones who will _ever_ know.*

And so / since we're all just / a bag of bones / on a rock / hurtling through space / and that all seems pretty reckless and scary / I've concluded that maybe that's why I involuntarily hold on to useless things like dates and memories / but I guess being a human is just inherently weird and heartbreaking and hard and stuff / and I suppose I'll never know for sure.

THE THINGS THEY CARRY

When I look out across this ocean you put between us,
I see two silent ships passing in the night.
I strain my eyes through the darkness,
watching closely for any shift in direction.
Nothing to see.
Nothing to hear.
All that I can make out
are my own lost signals,
waves gently lapping at steeled edges,
and two separate silhouettes,
one barely acknowledging the other,
only just enough to ensure they don't collide,
lest they disrupt all the things they carry.

TURKEY PANINI

the gelato freezer hums aggressively amidst
the clink of silverware on porcelain
a man orders a turkey panini
        "without the fig" — *what a waste.*

i sip my coffee and wonder if he lives his whole life like that —
devoid of the sweetest parts
choking down dry turkey
in the name of practicality.

NEW LINES FOR FORTUNE COOKIES

after Frank O'Hara

You'll be someone's trash and someone else's treasure. Don't mistake one for the other.

Falling feels like flying. Always pack a parachute.

Eliminate *should* from your vocabulary. Replace with, "What do I *want*?" Just be sure to have a vegetable every once in a while.

At some point, someone will flip the emergency shut-off valve on you. It will hurt like hell.

People will remember you by the perfume you wore ten years ago. You're allergic to it now.

That thing you're dealing with? Someone else is too. You're not that unique.

If you choose to die on that hill, make sure there's someone there to bury you.

Courageous conversations — have them.

Your heart is elastic. It's designed to stretch. Just brace yourself for when it snaps back at you. That shit stings.

Befriend your shadow. It has a lot to teach you. But definitely call bullshit on it from time to time.

Pedestals are not permanent resting places. Ever.

Someone will say, "*See you next time,*" and then proceed to walk out of your life. The door slamming will echo.

You will cry watching fireworks as the clock strikes midnight on New Year's Eve. Coldplay will be playing.

When in doubt, dance it out. Bonus points if the neighbors are watching.

Never underestimate the power of passion. It will prevail every time.

TAYLOR SWIFT SAID, "I WANT AURORAS AND SAD PROSE." AND AS FOR ME,

I want deep and meaningful relationships. Not mere surface level niceties, an occasional like on a photo, or a polite, but subdued *Happy Birthday* once a year. No.

I want closeness and connection. Unfiltered and raw. The kind where you fully show up as your flawed, imperfect self. The kind where someone really lets you in. The kind where someone sees you. All of you.

I want honest conversations about life and love and navigating the chaos, and how none of it makes sense, but how somehow all of it is beautiful. I want to hold space for the hard and the heavy. I want to find joy in the laughter and the lightness. I want inside jokes.

I want to muse about the Universe and the planets and the fault in our stars. I want to share memories and song lyrics and pictures of the sky. I want to unpack how none of it is a coincidence and how all of it matters. I want the tension to break. I want to vibe. I want knowing. I want ease.

I want a common understanding that cookie cutters only belong in the kitchen and have no business in shaping a life. I want to scream about how this existence isn't a recipe goddamnit, and you can't mix all the ingredients together and then expect to be able to separate them out because it doesn't work that way. It doesn't work.

I want the raw batter. I want the delicious mess. I want to scrape down the sides of the bowl and lick the spoon clean even though I know that's a roll of the dice (raw eggs and what not). But I don't care. I want to have my cake and eat it too.

I want to embrace the fervent hunger I was taught to suppress for so much of my life. Which is to say, I want it all. I want it all. I want it all.

15 WAYS TO STAY ALIVE

after Daphne Gottlieb

1. Plaster a smile to your face and clench your jaw until it aches.
   Call it *trying*.

2. Don't sleep. Toss and turn and play games with time. Become a creature
   of the night. Call it *remembering*.

3. Call your mom. Except for when you know you'll crumble the moment
   you hear her voice. In that case, don't call your mom. Call your *sister*.

4. Cry. In the car. On a walk. In the shower. In CVS on a Friday in December.
   Call it *cathartic*.

5. Run, walk, dance until you break your foot a second time. Tell yourself
   you won't let it happen again. Know you're probably lying. Call it *bad luck*.

6. Pray to the gods of sunshine, coffee, and music and bask in their
   therapeutic glory. Call it *mercy*.

7. Change the song immediately at the opening notes of *that song*. Call it
   protection.

8. Count effort by action, not by intention. Call it *experience*.

9. Sigh — deep and emptying. Wash, rinse, repeat. Call it *acceptance*.

10. Ignore the text messages coming through until you muster the capacity
    to engage. Call it *surviving*.

11. Laugh uncontrollably at the stupidest things. Call it *medicine*.

12. Lay on the floor and let your mind breathe. Call it *meditating*.

13. Make friends with your intuition. Allow the truth to speak. Even when
    it hurts. Call it *Knowing*.

14. Tell yourself everything works out the way it's meant to. Even when you
    don't believe it. Call it *trusting*.

15. String your own words together in an attempt to find peace. Call it *art*.

THE WORLD IS BURNING AND HEARTS ARE BREAKING AND ALL I CAN THINK ABOUT IS LOVE

And how I wonder if we'd be in this condition if we spent more time in school learning how to love one another instead of the countless hours spent learning how to solve for x, when sometimes there really is no logical answer.

All I can think about is where we'd be if everyone could put their fucking egos to the side and just let people be who they are.

All I can think about is how we might actually be able to move forward if people could acknowledge the darkness of yesterday and commit to bringing light to today.

All I can think about is how beautiful it could all be if everything wasn't mercilessly driven by power and money and control.

And I know that thinking about love isn't going to stop the terrible, isn't going to bring about change, but sometimes, when all reason fails, thinking about love feels like the most radical act of rebellion.

WE WIN THE WAR

In an alternate universe we win the war.
And by win, I mean,
we put the weapons down,
we break this stalemate,
we meet in the middle.
We join hands
and tilt our heads back
as the sky opens up
and washes away the blood and the pain,
returning the glow to our dirt-caked cheeks —
finally.

And we welcome it.

In an alternate universe we win the war.
And by win, I mean,
we finally *choose* to stop fighting.

NICE TO MEET YOU

after Molly Brodak and S. Lindsay

I am not a simple thing —
too deeply feeling.

You see,
I have shelves that store things,
too many things deemed "not good for me,"
that stockpile all the discarded items,
a nesting place for someone else's junk.
Shelves that end up tenderly caring for
all the stuff labeled 'useless' and 'impractical,'
making a home for the delicate.

I like to believe
I'm strong enough
to hold it all
and still stay afloat,
but sometimes,
sometimes
it just gets so heavy.

LIKE THAT

after Kim Addonizio

Love me like freshly shaved legs on just washed sheets. Like the indulgent cool of *both* a ceiling fan *and* a crisp breeze coming in through the window after a hot day in the sun.

Love me like the first sip of your favorite craft IPA at the end of a long, grueling day. Like one of your homemade espressos on a Sunday morning. Like an ice cold Topo Chico with lime. Love me like a half-baked chocolate chip cookie, gooey on the inside and not fully done, but all the more delicious that way.

Love me like you couldn't be wired more differently, but you could fix my shorted circuits any day. Like you're the electrician and the confidant and the co-pilot all in one.

Love me like I'm your favorite quirky mug, slightly discolored and chipped in a few places from wear and tear, but the perfect fit for your hands.

Love me like you could trace the constellation of birthmarks on my left cheek with your eyes closed. Like you could finish my sentences before I even open my mouth. Love me like it's subconscious, like it's without thinking. Love me like muscle memory.

Love me like solid ground and a soft place to land. Love me like, *"We'll figure it out together."*

Love me like you want the mess and the masterpiece even when there's paint all over the ground and the color scheme doesn't make sense (*it will never make sense*). Love me like nonsense is your second language, and I/we/us *is, always has been, always will be* your first.

Love me like it's just what you do. Love me *just the way you do.*

Just the way you do.

Yeah, love me like that.

IT'S TIME

"*It's time,*" he says over the roaring thrum of the airplane engine.
The stale air suddenly feels infinitely more suffocating as
my breath shortens,
my stomach sinks,
my heart quickens.
The pinpricks behind my eyes eagerly jump at the opportunity to dance
as salty tears waltz their way into my mask.
No altitude is high enough to lift me out of
these uncertainties I'm steeped in.

Because it's not time.
I don't know *when* it will be time.
I don't know *if* it will ever be time.
I don't know *if I even want it to...*

With those two simple words, my mind is off and racing.
With those two simple words, I feel the ironclad grip of time tighten,
continuing to squeeze the air out of my delicate, drifting balloon,
and I can't bear to think about
how long I have
until it pops.

NONSENSE

The thoughts rush in unannounced.

The

> *I shoulds and I shouldn'ts.*
> *I'm doing too much of this and not enough of that.*
> *I should feel ready at this point.*
> *I should embrace what's next.*
> *I should be able to let go of the things that fall through the*
> *cracks, instead of breaking my hands again and again trying*
> *to reach down to pull them out. Instead of killing myself*
> *bending over backwards, and for what?*

I know I should *lean into* the now,
but the weight of time and expectations
pins me down, and I resent the pull to concede this fight.
And when the pressure is mounting,
when I'm seeing stars,
when everything is swirling before me,
I just want it all to make sense.
But here in this chaos nothing makes sense

.

.

.

except you and me.

BOXES

"I mean you've checked all the boxes,
and I never want to ask you this in front of people but..."

And I die a little bit inside.
Because she means it with every bit of love in her body, she does.
But all I hear is: *This life has been reduced down to boxes.*

> *Checking boxes*
> *Burying things in boxes*
> *Making sure we stay within our own boxes*

I could scream.
But I don't.
Instead, I pull my *'Just Acceptable Enough for Company'* response out
of *its* rightful box,
nicely arrange it on a serving platter,
and politely offer it up.

SOULFIGHT

You play the opening notes of "Soulfight" by The Revivalists,
and I stop mid-chop.
Socked feet on the cold kitchen floor,
warmth flooding through me,
my furrowed brow softens,
and I can feel my dimples poke through.

I abandon whatever inner monologue I had been wrapped up in
because as your sound carries through the house,
more pressing matters are at hand —
I still can't decide if I like your version better on the guitar or the piano.

Truly, it doesn't matter.
All that matters is I like it,
and you know it.
So, you play.
For me.

Just like that, I'm taken by the melody.
And the battle cries of my own soul's fight
quiet down,
for now,
as I graciously let the music
drown it all out,
shut it all out,
and I exhale it all out,
resume my chopping,
and sing along.

LOOK AT THE STARS, LOOK HOW THEY SHINE FOR YOU

I drive to work on a Monday morning,
and somewhere between the toll road and Route 7 I'm taken.
Suddenly, I'm not strapped behind my steering wheel
rubbing the sleep from my eyes,
but standing,
high heels on patio stones,
like that time we stood,
chests thumping,
hearts pumping,
cheeks flushed from dancing,
gazing up under a blanket of stars,
the cold crush of winter's night a welcome departure
from the dizzying heat of the dance floor.
Coldplay's "Yellow" poured through the speakers,
fireworks lit up the sky,
and I cried,
for more reasons than I could ever begin to explain.

I leaned back into you,
felt your arms around me, and
I remember feeling
so many different things
rush through my body
in that moment.

And in this moment,
it all comes rushing back, and
isn't it just crazy how
it all comes rushing back,
turns me inside out
with just a couple of notes through my Nissan speakers?

But it always happens like this —
it never takes much
for it *all* to come rushing back.

PROGRESS

Despite the snail's pace of progress, I think I've rounded a corner.
But that doesn't mean I don't get turned around sometimes.
Like when the balmy nights transport me back to another place and time.
When the pulse of possibility zipped through my bloodstream,
a chemistry of rhythm and blues,
a karmic fire.

Back when defeat was just another word in the dictionary,
and not the soundtrack to this experience.
Back when blind faith led the way.
Back when I had the audacity to believe.

SIMPLE JOYS

a record spinning, crackling to a start / the sun finally breaking through perpetual gray / bare feet in the kitchen, swaying gently in loving arms / sunroof open, windows down driving, belting the bridge at the top of your lungs / Wednesday afternoon flowers for no apparent reason / the sweet juice of freshly picked strawberries running down your chin / the accomplished emptiness at the end of a solid run / the catharsis of good cry / cuddles / involuntarily dancing when the music just takes over your body / tracing the free-spirited path of a leaf unabashedly pirouetting to your feet / the gleeful shriek of tiny humans playing in sprinklers / the freedom of an empty calendar / a book you can't put down / an eruption of laughter that even you didn't expect / laying in bed on a planless Saturday morning, sun creeping through the curtains, listening to the birds chirping / the first sip of coffee / string lights draped over cobblestone streets / random I love you texts / lips brushing collarbone / a blanket of stars / fingertips trailing along the small of a back / a knowing twinkle in the eye of someone you love / finding exactly the right words / *"this made me think of you"* / perfect timing.

NOTES TO MY YOUNGER SELF

Most of us don't actually know what we're doing.

Human hearts and minds are the messiest things on this godforsaken planet.

It's completely okay and even necessary to rethink things you once believed.

Life is made up of seasons. Everything is temporary. Even when it doesn't feel like it.

Healing is not linear. It looks different for everyone.

Sometimes things are about function and sometimes they're about feeling, and if we're lucky, we can find things that give us both.

Let your journey be your own — free from judgment — specifically, yours.

Mental and emotional suffering can and will lead to physical suffering. Do what you have to do to take care of your whole self first. The rest can wait.

Music is medicine, laughter heals, and dancing cures all. Every time.

If people truly want you in their life, they will make space. And if they don't, they won't. Because circumstantial complexities aside, it's really that simple. Things are figureoutable if you truly want them to be.

Find your things. The things that ground you, revive you, save you, light you up. Pour your passion and pain into them like your life depends on it. It kind of does.

Sensitivity is a superpower.

Energy doesn't lie. Trust the vibes you get.

Some things just don't and won't ever make sense to you. You don't have to like them, but surrender to a greater wisdom and save yourself the headache/heartache in trying to figure it all out. They will never add up perfectly, no matter how many times you try.

99% of the time, it's "both/and" — shades of gray versus black and white.

People change their mind. And there is nothing you can do about it.

Communication is really the secret ingredient for pretty much everything. Cut that off and watch things crumble.

Tomorrow is never guaranteed. Speak your mind. Say how you feel. Tell people you love them. Do the things that make you happy, even when they seem crazy. If you want something, go after it.

You will get hurt. And it will suck. But take the risks anyway.

Know who you can call and fall apart to, no matter how major or trivial your issues feel. No matter how many times you've had the same conversations over and over and over.

Shared experience/emotion is a powerful glue that bonds people together in the most unexpected ways.

One of the best strategies for getting out of your own way is to simply help another human. When you're hurting, love harder. There's always someone who could use it.

Bodies are meant to change.

Words are just words until they're held up by actions.

We're all just main charactering our way through this crazy place. Don't take things too personally. Most of the time it's not about you. It's about them. Preserve your energy.

Certain things are always going to be painful. And that's okay. You are a human, not a robot. You're allowed to have soft spots.

FEEL YOUR DAMN FEELINGS.

Silence speaks volumes.

Be unapologetically you. The right people will find you. The right people will stay.

WE DON'T TALK ENOUGH ABOUT HOW

driving with the windows down
in 70 degree weather,
alone, but for the songs
pouring through our speakers,
soothes the soul like it's some kind of holy.

we don't talk enough
about how the sky becomes
a wistful watercolor
to match our spirits;
the words and the wind
and the warmth of the sunset
all speaking for us
as if to say,
"I'm not there yet, but I'm on my way."

GALACTIC

She tells me that my soul is galactic,
and therefore I will never truly feel at home here,
whatever '*here*' means in this vast unknown.

On a soul level, I understand completely
in a way that words would prove I do not.
Yet for once,
for just this once,
my words don't matter,
but everything makes sense.

CYCLES

I'm just not sure what to make of it —
the fragility of things,
the transience of this life
that we all take so seriously,
the cyclical nature of the
building and breaking,
bending, upending,
only for us to rise again,
changed,
different.

We come undone,
unraveled, unmoored,
continuously losing precious fibers of our being,
and we think
how can we possibly learn to
exist
like this?
But then we do.

And that's how it goes —

this constant undoing and redoing,
endlessly relearning how to
put one foot in front of the other
on often not so solid ground.
Teetering,
tottering,
at times gracelessly wobbling,
yet somehow,
somehow,
finding our way.

About the Author

As it turns out, her mind is an endless wonder wheel and she's terrible at sitting still. She'll be the first to tell you that she's actually her worst self when she's tired and hungry, so don't say you haven't been warned. She'll swear she's going to "get to bed early" every single night, and then despite being exhausted, she'll stay up late anyway. She hates that she does this.

Truthfully, eyes are the first thing she notices about a person because she knows they reveal more than people want to believe. She finds endless awe in the sky — she'll stop whenever and wherever she is to admire it. She thinks the world would be a sweeter place if we all looked to it more often.

If you look closely, you'll see her heart on her sleeve and the truth in her eyes. You'll see rainbows and rainstorms, clear skies and thunderclouds. You'll see her laughing *and* crying. You'll see her dancing.

Tenacity aside, the truth is, she's a lover not a fighter. But make no mistake she will fight and fight hard for the things she wants, for the things she loves. She considers that *mostly* good.

She'd scream it from the rooftops if she could, that she deeply wishes the world was defined by less boxes and more overlapping spheres. Nostalgia is her Achilles' heel. It gets her every time. She wholeheartedly believes that hugs from the right people are one of the best things you can get.

Although she might not always show it, she's sometimes scared to share her art. But she's learned that usually the scary things are the very things we need to do. So, she does it anyway. It pushes her to grow.

She occasionally worries that all the things that make her "*her*" are too tiresome for anyone to possibly deal with. But she remembers that the right people will want to. She doesn't fret over it much.

She's learning that living a life is less of arriving at a destination and more of a never-ending journey with a lot of bumps in the road.

She's working on making peace with the difficult things, the things that are hard to swallow. It, like her, like most things, is a work in progress.

Acknowledgements

A number of pieces included in this collection were influenced by some extremely talented individuals, many of whom I've had the privilege of encountering through the online writing community. I am endlessly inspired by and grateful for these incredible writers. Their brilliance sparks ideas for my own writing on a regular basis, and their camaraderie and support help fuel my growth as a writer. Whether I found inspiration in a prompt they put out, or felt compelled to write a poem after an original piece or line of their own, I want to extend my utmost gratitude to each of them. They are the truth tellers, the storytellers, and the creative souls who continue to use words to shed light on the good, the bad, the ugly, and everything in between. A very special thank you to them and all the amazing art they put out into the world.

Amy Kay // @amykaypoetry
Michelle Awad // @theconstantpoet
Nick Olah // @nick.olah.poetry
Angelea Lowes // @angelealowes
Bella Townsend // @poems.by.bella
Claire Donohoe // @cwroteit
Lex Cherniak // @accpoems
Jess Janz // @jessjanz
Ana Dee // @ana.dee.writes
Kim Addonizio // @kimaddonizio
S. Lindsay // @lindsay_poetry
Eliza // @poetry.by.eliza
Kim McKellar // @kimmckellar_poetry
Daphne Gottlieb
Frank O'Hara
Molly Brodak
Taylor Swift // @taylorswift
Wild Rivers // @wildriversmusic
F. Scott Fitzgerald
Ada Limón // @adalimonwriter
Nikki Giovanni // @giovanni.nikki

Mosaic

Mosaic, Shelby Kardon's debut poetry collection, was published in October 2020 and is available on Amazon in print and ebook.

We're all essentially mosaics. Living collections of small pieces that combine to make something incredible. *Mosaic* is a collection of poems that highlights the beautiful, difficult, and often confusing aspects of finding our way into adulthood. Aspects that combine to create the imperfect and ever-changing masterpiece that we are. *Mosaic* is a revelation that we can't outrun life and all of its complexity. It's an understanding that it all matters. It's an exploration of moments, emotions, and earlier selves, and how they shape us into who we are. It underscores how everything we experience and everything we feel makes us unique, while also connecting us. Our mosaic is what makes us who we are. Our mosaic is what makes us human.

Follow Shelby Kardon on Instagram
@mosaic_poems

CPSIA information can be obtained
at www.ICGtesting.com
Printed in the USA
BVHW030334101122
651448BV00013B/957